The Microlight Pilot's
Handbook

8th edition

D1073631

To

Capt. Julian Doswell

for his patience and guidance in
contributing to this book

With thanks to:

Peter Coles – for the initial suggestion
of a new approach

Geoff Weighell and Guy Gratton – for
those tips and reminders on
occasions

Also with appreciation to David Young
together with David Garrison and
Fiona Luckhurst for their
contributions to the latest edition

The Microlight Pilot's
Handbook

8th edition

APPROVED
BY
BMAA
PANEL OF
EXAMINERS

Brian Cosgrove

Airlife

First published in 1986 by
Airlife Publishing, an imprint of
The Crowood Press Ltd
Ramsbury, Marlborough
Wiltshire SN8 2HR

enquiries@crowood.com

www.crowood.com

Eighth revised edition 2013

This impression 2020

British Library Cataloguing in Publication Data
A catalogue record for this book is available from the British Library

ISBN 978 1 84797 509 6

The publisher would like to thank Julian Doswell and David Young for their assistance in producing the eighth revised edition.

Cover pictures courtesy P&M Aviation (front and back top left), and Kemble Flying Club (back top right and bottom).

A percentage of the royalties from sales of this book is being donated to the BMAA Young Persons Training Bursary.

Illustrations by David Barber

Typeset by Asgard Publishing Services, Leeds

Printed and bound in Malaysia by Times Offset (M) Sdn Bhd

Contents

The Author

From designing, building and flying model aircraft in the 1930s through service with the Air Defence Cadet Corps, Air Training Corps and Royal Air Force in the 1940s, the author has always had an affinity for aeroplanes since a first flight at the age of seven.

1942 saw his involvement as a pupil in the opening days of ATC gliding where solo training in open primary types was the norm – shades of the earlier types of microlights to come 40 years later.

After wartime service with the RAF in the UK and Far East as a meteorologist on the ground and in the air, the early post-war years were spent as a gliding instructor culminating in an RAF 'A' Star Category in both solo and dual methods of training.

Having become involved with microlights in 1979, he predicted that total freedom for microlighting would be short-lived, and work began on ideas for the inevitable control to come. Reading matter for ground studies appeared in the form of *Ultra Light Aircraft and the Air*, followed by *Microlight Aircraft and the Air* when the aircraft name was later changed to meet with impending CAA legislation.

By then a BMAA Council member, a start was made on preparing future pilot licence examinations specific to microlights. These were accepted by the CAA and a rapport was established which was to grow over future years.

In 1983, now in a full-time role with the BMAA, and a few months later its chief executive, negotiations continued with the CAA on many aspects of pilot licensing and instructor rating. Also, airworthiness procedures were set up and safeguards put in place for existing aeroplanes threatened with grounding by airworthiness standards yet to be introduced.

After retirement in May 1993 he became an independent consultant with the BMAA, among other clients, particularly on site planning matters until August 2002.

The author was awarded the Ashley Doubtfire Trophy in 1985 for Services to Microlight Aviation, and in 1990 was elected a Freeman of the Guild of Air Pilots and Air Navigators. In 1993 came election as a Fellow of the Royal Meteorological Society and the award of an MBE in the Queen's Birthday Honours List. In 2002 he received a Royal Aero Club Silver Medal. Brian became President of the BMAA and continued his close links with the Association until his death in June 2010. His unique position and lasting legacy has been affectionately described as: 'Brian Cosgrove – The Father of Microlighting'.

Author Aloft!
Among the UK's first single-seater 3-axis types, this machine was very much liked by those who flew it – with or without the cockpit cover!

Chapter 1
Introduction

Although the presentation of this eighth edition is entirely new in approach, it still contains the same content – the 'need to know' information you require. It is hoped that the introduction of colour pictures, particularly in the case of clouds, will contribute to an easier understanding of the points being made. It is said that a picture speaks a thousand words!

Although the microlight may make satisfying that 'dream' to fly much closer than it has ever been, the knowledge to do so remains similar in many aspects to the standards required for flying conventional light aeroplanes. In fact it could be quite justifiably argued that the standards must be greater in some respects in view of the ordinary fields from which the microlight can operate.

The aim of this book is not just to prepare you for passing the National Private Pilots Licence examinations as an end in itself, but to provide you with a real understanding and recognition of those factors which influence safe flight for you and passengers who will fly with you in the future – be it in a microlight or in any other form of aircraft. The principles are the same.

The chapters you need to digest for the exams are listed in the panel below:

This eighth edition of the book continues to fulfil the aim to update where necessary. Particular attention is still paid to those aspects of Air Law where the microlight aeroplane may be operating under exemptions from the law laid down in the Air Navigation Order. Such exemptions are unlikely to be covered in other publications on Air Law but they still require legal compliance and the pilot must have knowledge of them.

Throughout the book, where information is considered to be of interest, but not necessarily essential, the text is in a pink box.

As before, the subject of how to fly the aeroplane has been left where it belongs – in the hands of your flying instructor. However, if you digest the information presented to you here, you and your instructor will have a much easier ride.

Brian Cosgrove

3	Principles of Flight	Why and how your aeroplane can fly
4	Power and Ancillaries	How to ensure it will stay in flight
5	Basic Flight Instruments	Monitoring your control of flight
6	Air Law	The rules to obey as a pilot
7	Human Performance Limitations	Your mind and body for safe flight
8	Meteorology	The environment in which you fly
9	Navigation	How to find your way before you fly
10	Flight Planning and Map reading	Planning and then finding your way as you fly

Chapter 2
Aeroplane Types

Unlike its 'big brother' the light aeroplane, the microlight can appear in a variety of types. The early ones in the UK mainly stemmed from the USA, which waded into the world of aluminium/Dacron to re-invent the aeroplane. The use of composite materials was also to be seen at times. Not only did the appearance seem strange, but the control systems could also be quite intriguing! Over 'the pond' they were called Ultralights. Just as with vintage cars, some of these 'oldies' can still be seen flying on occasion.

Powered Hang Glider

Above: The beginning of the microlight in the UK – an engine added to a hang glider in the late 1970s to early 1980s.

Flexwing (Weight-shift) Microlight

Above: The flexwing trike was to become the major UK type of microlight. Here is a single-seater from the early days arriving at John O'Groats after a flight from Land's End!

Below: The advent of Permit to Fly legislation allowed the introduction of two-seater microlights. The ability to carry an instructor transformed the interest in microlight flying.

The P&M Quik is typical of the modern breed of high-performance flexwing microlights, with capabilities similar to those of many small light aircraft. P&M AVIATION

Right: *The Magic Cyclone is a single-seat flexwing, offering cheap and enjoyable flying with a minimum of fuss. P&M AVIATION*

Ancient Hybrids

A mixture of weight shift and aerodynamic control. This aeroplane from the USA was very prominent in the UK in the early 1980s. It had a reputation for being 'unstallable'.

Fixed-wing (2- or 3-axis)

Yes! This Canadian design is twin-engined. Fortunately a blind eye was turned to the need for a twin-rating when UK microlight pilot licences came into being.

One of the few microlights you had to climb up to enter the cockpit. It was a two-seater used for a time as a trainer – there are still some about kept by dedicated enthusiasts.

Here we have an unusual but interesting 2-axis machine. Pitch control is achieved by moving the entire upper wing, on which there are no ailerons. The rudder is operated by sideways movement of the control column wheel.

The Ikarus C42 (left) and Flight Design CTSW have the looks and performance of a light aircraft, yet are still classed as microlights and can be flown by the NPPL (M) holder. CLEARPROP! MICROLIGHT SCHOOL (LEFT) AND P&M AVIATION (RIGHT)

Powered Parachute – Trike Unit and Foot-launched

Instead of a wing with a framework, these two-seater trikes use a ram-air inflated canopy. A pilot's licence is required.

A simple paramotor outfit. Because take-off and landing are on foot, it can be operated with a minimum of regulation.

Powered Hang Glider

Here we are, back to square one after many years. Some pilots have reacted to the sophistication and consequent cost of most current microlights by returning to simplicity. No doubt the Foot Launched Microlight (FLM) will find its niche in the sport.

Chapter 3
Principles of Flight

The Basics

Learning to fly a microlight relates to handling the various controls and becoming aware of their effect on your flight path. However, prior to mastering the practical aspects of flight, the 'complete' pilot should in the first place be aware of why the aeroplane can fly.

This chapter covers the microlight types most in use nowadays. However, for those who may be fascinated by the control systems of the past (and in case of their possible return in the future!) they are given coverage under a 'want to know' insert in a pink box .

The Aerofoil

Flight is possible because a wing can generate lift and it does so in two ways.

– By the angle at which it meets the **Airflow** – known as the **Angle of Attack** in relation to the chord line of the wing.

– By the shape of the wing section from front to back – **Leading Edge** to **Trailing Edge**. This shape is known as the **Aerofoil Section** and is generally flattish on the bottom and curved on the top. This curve is known as **Camber** and later you will see how camber contributes around two-thirds of the total lift produced. The **Datum Line** through an aerofoil section is known as the **Chord Line**.

Basic terms in bold above are to be seen in Figure 3.1.

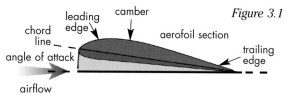

Figure 3.1

leading edge — camber — aerofoil section
chord line
angle of attack — trailing edge
airflow

Airspeed

A cambered wing set at an angle of attack will not in itself create lift. When you watch an aircraft take off you will see that at first it accelerates along the ground until at a particular point it parts company with 'mother earth' and flies.

What happens is this. The forward movement causes air to flow over the wing and it is this flow of air called **Airspeed** that produces the lift. The greater the airspeed the greater is the lift that the wing will generate.

When the airspeed is sufficient to produce enough lift for flight the aircraft is said to have reached **Flying Speed**.

Angle of Attack

Consider now the angle of attack and its contribution to lift. As the airflow meets the wing leading edge it divides to pass under and over the aerofoil.

Figure 3.2

In Figure 3.2 above you can see how the air passing underneath is deflected downwards. This in turn creates an opposite effect in that the aerofoil is pushed up. In fact it creates one-third of total lift.

Take a piece of card and swing it around at arm's length making sure that you hold it at an angle as you do so. You will find that the card will try to lift out of your hand and the faster you swing it the more it tries to rise.

The airflow deflected down by the Angle of Attack produces a **Resultant** upward force (Figure 3.3).

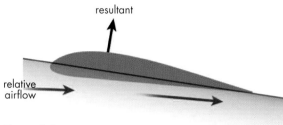

Figure 3.3

Camber

Next let us consider the contribution made to total lift by camber.

The air moving over the top cambered surface has further to travel than the air passing underneath and speeds up to do so.

Picture a river flowing sedately along being suddenly faced with a restriction. The given amount of water speeds up in order to pass through the restriction without causing a build up behind. It will be going at its fastest at the narrowest point.

A scientist called Bernoulli found that the faster a fluid went through such a restriction then the less became the pressure it exerted on the sides of that restriction (Figure 3.4).

Look carefully at the shape of the sides of the restriction. Remove one side, say the top one, and you will see a curved surface closely resembling the cambered surface of an aerofoil.

Now air behaves as a fluid and as it speeds up over the camber the pressure exerted on that top surface will decrease as per Bernoulli's findings.

Naturally if pressure on the top decreases it makes pressure below become relatively greater; in consequence the aerofoil is pushed up. This reduction in pressure produces double the resultant force generated by air being deflected down, i.e. two-thirds of the total lift generated (Figure 3.5).

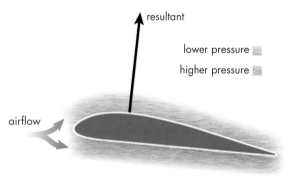

Figure 3.5

Whereas cambered aerofoils are usually of rigid construction, this does not apply to the powered parachute. This type of aeroplane does not use the round type of canopy with which some people are familiar. It uses a **ram-air** type of canopy composed of a number of individual cells linked to each other by vents. This allows a rapid and uniform inflation when the open front of the canopy is faced into wind or moves forward into the airflow. When inflated, an aerofoil section is formed which generates lift enabling the machine to glide and fly like a conventional aeroplane (Figure 3.6).

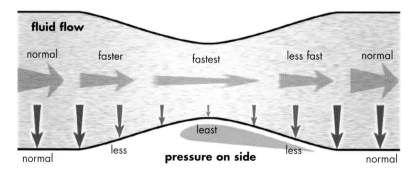

Figure 3.4

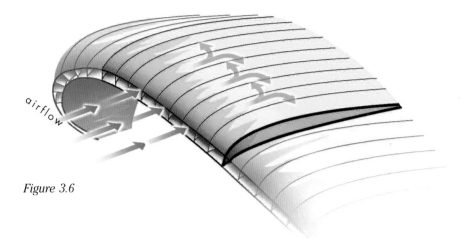

Figure 3.6

Prove the effect of camber for yourself. Take a piece of paper and blow onto it so that your breath hits the top of the leading edge. You will see the paper rise in the airflow caused by your breath (Figure 3.7).

Figure 3.7

Forces at Play

In beginning to talk about forces it is worth spending a moment or two gaining an understanding as to what takes place when a force is applied or created.

An object rests at point A and on moving it along in direction B one can say that a 'Force' provided the movement (Figure 3.8).

Figure 3.8

The same can be said if the object is moved in direction C (Figure 3.9).

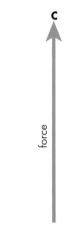

Figure 3.9

Simultaneously exert forces B and C from A, vertically and horizontally, and the object will move to D like an arrow from a bow at an angle of 45° (Figure 3.10).

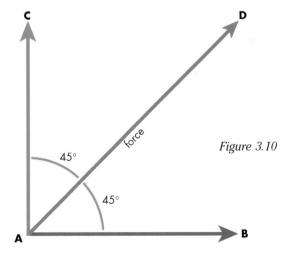

Figure 3.10

Now think of Figure 3.10 as a parallelogram – a shape where opposite sides and angles are equal to one another.

The diagonal A to D is the total force produced; but the object can be said to have moved part horizontally and part vertically in arriving at D.

Thus the force towards D can be said to have two components – one horizontal (A to B) and the other, vertical (A to C).

These two forces are represented by the sides of the parallelogram projecting from the start of the diagonal at A. (Figure 3.11).

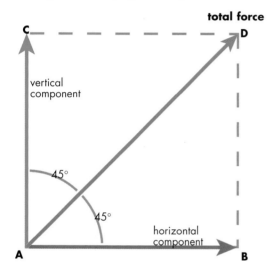

Figure 3.11

As the angle of the diagonal is the same between each side, the length of AB is the same as AC. In other words, the horizontal force and the vertical force are equal. Prove this by measuring them for yourself.

But what if the diagonal varies in angle? The picture may be thus. (Figure 3.12).

In (a) the horizontal component H is 1.72 times as much as the vertical one V.

In (b) the opposite is the case.

You can now see that given a resultant force (a diagonal) it is possible to establish the value of its components by measurement alone – unless you are a trigonometry addict!

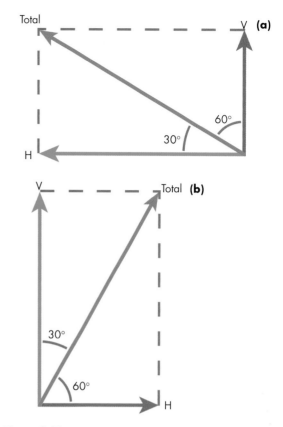

Figure 3.12

Once again, try it for yourself (Figure 3.13).

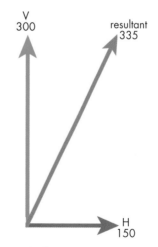

Figure 3.13

The principle we have just discussed is known as the **Parallelogram of Forces**.

No apologies are offered for this slight incursion into mathematics because in grasping this you will be well equipped to understand the forces at play in flight.

The Four Forces in Flight

There will be many forces to face as this book progresses. Let's start with the four basic forces at play when an aeroplane flies.

Weight

Acts vertically down (gravity) and has to be overcome by a force acting vertically upwards so that flight may be sustained. It is basically constant in flight except for a decrease taking place with the usage of fuel.

Lift

Acts upwards to overcome weight. It will vary according to airspeed and/or angle of attack. It acts at right angles to the airflow, but not necessarily in exact opposition to weight when out of straight and level flight, as you are about to see.

Thrust

Produces the forward movement to provide an airflow over the wing. It will vary according to the power applied and/or the angle of attack.

Drag

The force which tends to hold back or resist forward movement. It will vary with airspeed and angle of attack and acts in opposition to thrust.

The four forces are depicted in Figure 3.14 below.

Equilibrium

An aircraft maintaining constant height at a constant speed will have Lift exactly equal to Weight (no climb or descent) and Thrust will be exactly equal to Drag (no acceleration or deceleration).

In this state the aircraft is said to be in **equilibrium**.

Out of Straight Flight

Equilibrium assumes straight and level flight. While on the subject of the four forces, it is worth looking at the picture when the aeroplane is not in this situation. Also keep in mind the parallelogram of forces discussed earlier.

You will recall that lift acts at a right angle to the airflow over the wing and is equal to weight in straight and level flight at constant speed. (Figure 3.15a below).

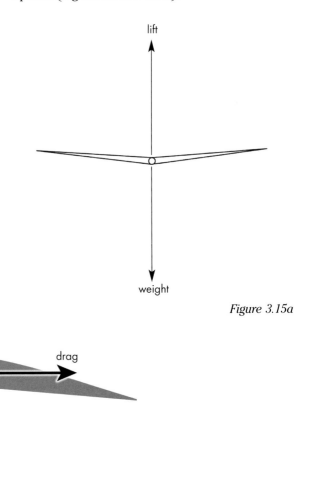

Figure 3.15a

Figure 3.14

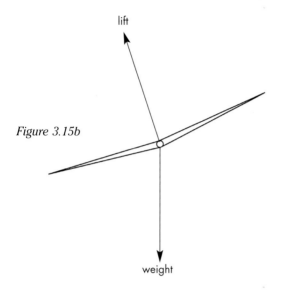

Figure 3.15b

The aeroplane now rolls to one side and the lift force is no longer vertical – it is now at an angle (Figure 3.15b above). Using a parallelogram of forces you will see two components related to the lift force at its new angle. There is now a horizontal force 'pulling' inwards which causes the aeroplane to turn (Figure 3.15c below)

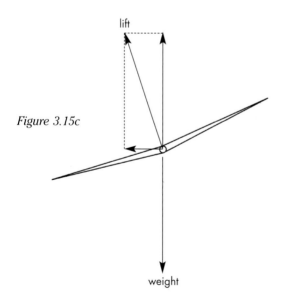

Figure 3.15c

Also, as mentioned earlier, the lift force is no longer opposite the weight; but, more importantly, you can also see that the value of the vertical component of the lift force is now less than the weight.

Drag

Drag needs some amplification as it comes in two distinct types.

Induced Drag

The first type is directly linked with the production of lift.

We talked earlier about the angle of attack at which the aerofoil meets the airflow and how this deflected the airflow downwards.

The resultant upwards force, acting at right angles to this downward flow, is 'bent' back out of the vertical and at once produces two components.

The vertical one we already know to be lift. The horizontal one acts rearwards and is naturally a drag component. It is known as **Induced Drag**. (Figure 3.16).

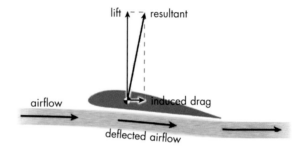

Figure 3.16

It is now appropriate to look at what is happening on the creation of induced drag.

The unequal pressure distribution which enables a wing to produce lift also produces this drag. The increased pressure below the wing tries to equalise with the decreased pressure on the top surface, and it does so at the wing tips (Figure 3.17).

■ lower pressure
■ higher pressure

Figure 3.17

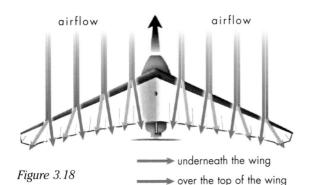

airflow   airflow

Figure 3.18

→ underneath the wing

→ over the top of the wing

This movement results in a two-directional flow of air – outwards underneath the wing and inwards over the top. The shift in direction is most pronounced towards the tips (Figure 3.18 above).

When the two airstreams meet there is a cross-flow situation which results in the formation of a spiral flow known as a trailing edge vortex.

The numerous trailing edge vortices so formed end up moving towards each tip to create two main wing-tip vortices (Figure 3.19 below).

Any disturbance to the smooth flow of air will naturally cause drag. In this case it cannot be avoided as where lift is produced so is induced drag.

Attempts are made to reduce the vortex effect by the use of wings of long span related to a narrow chord – usually associated with sailplanes.

Side-tracking drag for a moment, you may as well know of the term used for describing the relationship of span to chord.

It is called **Aspect Ratio** and is a figure derived from dividing the span by the chord.

See how wings of similar area can have entirely different aspect ratios (Figure 3.20).

AR=20/5=**4**   AR=50/2=**25**

Figure 3.20

Wings of low aspect ratio are usually associated with fighter or aerobatic aircraft where rapid manoeuvrability is the order of the day but plenty of power is available to deal with the induced drag.

High aspect ratio wings are very much confined to sailplanes where minimum drag is critical in the absence of power and the need for minimum sink and maximum penetration count for everything.

Parasite Drag

Progress has brought about an adjustment in the terminology for drag. For example, **Parasite Drag** is the term now used to embrace all forms of drag other than the Induced type. Let's take the first one.

The first type of drag is caused by the aircraft itself. Any object moving through air or water will experience a resistance to such movement.

Walking against a wind is an example you must be used to. Do this with a fully opened umbrella in front of you and you will be left with no doubt.

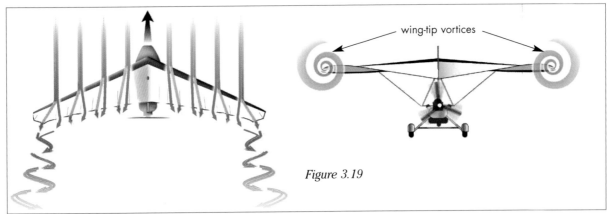

wing-tip vortices

Figure 3.19

The same effect is experienced by an aircraft as it is propelled through the air. This resistance is known as **Form Drag** and it is reduced as far as possible by streamlining (Figure 3.21).

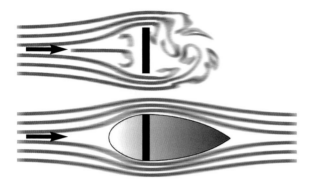

Figure 3.21

The second type occurs when, although you may have a nice streamlined machine, if the surface is rough it will increase overall drag; this type is known as **Skin Friction**. On many occasions you can see pilots polishing their 'steed' to reduce this factor – particularly at competitive events.

A third type stems from the turbulence caused by additional items which are not specifically involved in the flight of the aeroplane but protrude out into the airflow. A perfect example would be the gun turrets on the nose and upper or lower part of the fuselage of World War II bombers. Often these 'sore thumb' additions were removed for special operations where speed was crucial.

But back to the matter in hand.

To those who may think that the open front of a powered parachute canopy is likely to cause considerable drag, in actual fact there is a **back pressure** created by the air in the inflated wing which produces an invisible leading edge (Figure 3.22).

Figure 3.22

Total Drag
The amount of drag produced by an aircraft in flight varies with airspeed. At **low** airspeeds parasite drag is at a minimum whereas Induced drag will be at a maximum, but it will reduce rapidly as airspeed increases.

Total Drag, embracing both Induced and Parasite Drag, will be minimal at an airspeed between the two airspeeds mentioned above.

The relationship between drag and airspeed is best shown by the simple graph in Figure 3.23.

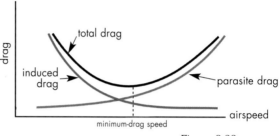

Figure 3.23

Speed Squared Law
For those mathematically inclined, Form Drag is proportional to the square of the speed.

You may have noticed that when increasing speed on a bicycle the resistance (drag) becomes so much greater than you expected.

The reason is that when you double your speed the drag created is **four** times as much. Treble your speed and drag is **nine** times more; ten times the speed and drag is **one hundred** times greater.

This 'Pearl of Wisdom' is known as the **Speed Squared Law**.

Now this law applies equally to lift as it does to drag. In other words, if you double the speed you produce four times the lift – and so on.

Varying the Angle of Attack
The angle of attack is the angle at which the wing meets the **Airflow** and it can vary according to the way you fly your aircraft.

As the angle of attack is increased so is the speed of the airflow over the top. At the same time a decrease of speed occurs on the underside of the wing. The pressure difference between top and bottom discussed earlier is thus widened and the upward force is increased.

However, as the angle increases the resultant force produced is 'leaning' further back with only a partial increase in the lift component but a substantial increase of induced drag (Figure 3.24).

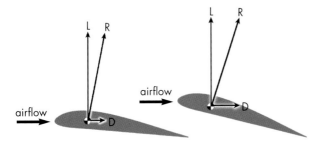

Figure 3.24

As long as there is sufficient power to maintain the same airspeed, increasing the angle of attack will produce more lift but only up to a point. More on this later.

Climb too steeply with insufficient power to cope and although your wing may be pointing upwards, as you slow down the aircraft will just 'mush' and the actual flight path will be nearly horizontal as it can climb no more (Figure 3.25).

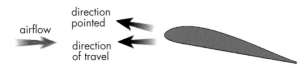

Figure 3.25

This configuration is suitable for the situation where you wish to fly slowly without loss of height. However, it can be a critical position to put yourself in and why this can be so will be made clear when 'stalling' is discussed shortly.

Alternatively, you feel you are descending too fast and without applying any extra power you raise the nose of the aircraft in order to slow down. Once again if the power is insufficient to take you along your chosen flight path the aircraft will 'mush' and the flight path will be different from the direction in which the wing is pointing (Figure 3.26).

Figure 3.26

Remember, the angle of attack is the angle at which the wing meets the airflow and not the direction in which it is pointing. Once the angle reaches a critical point and that point is exceeded then lift breaks down.

The Stall

For the aerofoil to produce lift efficiently the flow of air over its surface must be smooth and unbroken. Being endowed with the properties of a fluid there is a tendency for the particles of air to stick to the aerofoil. However, there is a breaking point (Figure 3.27).

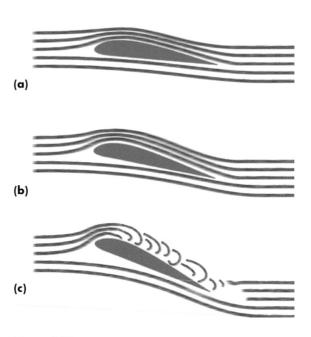

Figure 3.27

Situations (a) and (b) show the aerofoil at different angles of attack with the airflow behaving as it should do.

However, in situation (c) the angle has become too steep for the air to cling to the upper surface any longer and it breaks away thus destroying the smooth flow and the reduction in pressure which provides the major part of total lift.

In short, the wing is said to have **stalled** and the airspeed at which this occurs is known as the **Stalling Speed**. If your airspeed is allowed to drop too low your angle of attack will have become too high and up to two-thirds of the total lift will go at the stall. The angle at which this occurs is around 15°.

The behaviour of an aircraft in a stall will vary according to the type of aircraft. Broadly speaking the pattern is this. At the point of stall the nose will drop and as the aircraft takes up the nose-down attitude the airspeed will begin to build up. On reaching flying speed normal flight can be resumed.

The critical issue about the stall is the loss of height when the aircraft is in the stalled condition combined with the loss of height involved during the recovery process.

The stalling speed for a given aeroplane may be set at a certain figure. However, the same aeroplane can be made heavier or lighter according to the amount of fuel/passengers carried.

If heavier, an above normal airspeed will be needed to produce the extra lift required. If lighter, the less lift required means flight can be maintained at below normal airspeed so the stalling speed can vary.

Another point you must watch: Where the stalling speed is greater, the longer will be your take-off or landing run.

Safe airspeed is one of the most vital things to watch in flight. Maintaining sufficient airspeed keeps the angle of attack below the stalling angle.

'Thrust' with no Power
The question might be running through your mind as to where an aircraft with no engine can obtain 'thrust' in order to produce airspeed. The answer is best given with a simple analogy first and a technical explanation afterwards.

A railway truck standing on a level track will not move forward until an engine comes along to push or pull it. However, place the truck on a sloping track and on releasing the brake it will roll downhill unaided.

So it is with an aircraft with no engine (or

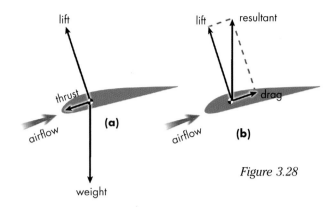

Figure 3.28

engine off). It uses gravity to provide thrust. Also, by adopting a nose-down attitude lift now acts forwards as well as upwards. This combined with weight produces a forward force or hypothetical 'Thrust' (Figure 3.28a). At the same time it can be seen how in this attitude drag contributes to produce a resultant upwards force opposite to weight which is greater than lift (Figure 3.28b).

Lift/Drag Ratio
At a given airspeed and angle of attack a wing will produce a certain amount of lift together with a certain amount of drag.

The relationship between the two is called the **Lift/Drag Ratio**.

If the lift generated happens to be 10 times the drag then the Lift/Drag Ratio is said to be 10:1.

Every aeroplane has an airspeed at which the angle of attack will produce the maximum amount of lift for the minimum amount of drag.

Knowing that particular airspeed is crucial should you ever find yourself with no engine and the need to reach a safe landing ground some way ahead. It is at this airspeed that you will cover the maximum distance before arriving on 'Mother Earth'.

Reducing airspeed with the idea of staying up longer to cover a greater distance is not on. The increased angle of attack this brings about may increase lift and thus a reduced rate of sink; but, there will also be an increase in drag which will reduce the Lift/Drag Ratio and so reduce the distance you can cover in the time remaining in the air.

Figure 3.29

L/D at maximum – best airspeed

airfield

40 mph

50 mph

30 mph

Increasing airspeed to arrive there before running out of height will also not work. The increase in airspeed requires a decrease in angle of attack which also brings about a decrease in lift. Although drag may reduce as well, the amount is not enough to prevent yet again, a reduced Lift/Drag Ratio. Examples of the three situations can be seen in Figure 3.29 above.

Best Gliding Angle
You will no doubt eventually come across the term 'best gliding angle' – again expressed as a ratio, say 10:1. This is only another way of saying that the aeroplane will travel 10 feet forward for every 1 foot of height lost.

Flying at the best gliding angle assumes you will be flying at the best airspeed – that which provides the maximum lift/drag ratio.

For the glide angle to be at its best in practical terms presupposes you are flying in still air. Given a headwind the angle in relation to the ground will be steeper; with a tailwind it becomes more shallow.

Whilst mathematically difficult to demonstrate, you can increase speed in a headwind and decrease same in a tailwind to achieve maximum distance.

Minimum Sink
Whilst flying at an airspeed below a value that provides the best gliding angle is not a good idea in relation to travelling distance, there can be times when it is useful. There is an airspeed a little less than the best gliding value, but not so low that drag has started to increase significantly, called the minimum sink airspeed. Flying at this airspeed will keep you

in the air the longest whilst maximising your 'thinking time'.

Best Rate of Climb and Best Angle of Climb
The handling instructions for many aeroplanes give two climbing air speeds for the aeroplane concerned.

– Best Rate of Climb

– Best Angle of Climb

There is a difference between the two though you may be forgiven if at first you think this is not so.

Best rate of climb refers to attaining the maximum amount of height in the minimum amount of time at maximum power. The manual will give you an airspeed at which to fly to achieve this rate.

Now, it may be that the angle of climb that this rate involves is insufficient to clear an obstruction on your take-off path.

To cater for such a situation the manual gives you the best angle of climb airspeed at which to fly. This airspeed will be lower than for 'Best Rate' but the angle of climb will be greater.

By flying more slowly it takes longer to reach the obstruction, but in the extra time bought enough height is reached to clear it even though the rate of climb itself is reduced.

Using hypothetical figures the situation is depicted in Figure 3.30 on page 23.

If you are really keen, measure it for yourself. On the other hand you would do better listening to guidance from your instructor on obstruction clearance rather than becoming immersed in theory.

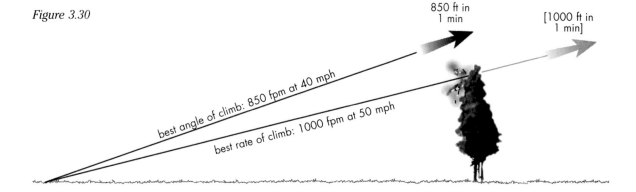

Figure 3.30

850 ft in
1 min

[1000 ft in
1 min]

best angle of climb: 850 fpm at 40 mph

best rate of climb: 1000 fpm at 50 mph

On no account in normal circumstances should you be taking off from any site with an obstruction that warrants the above assessment. If you are forced to land in such a place it would be better to dismantle the aeroplane rather than take off and dismantle yourself.

Varying the Angle of Attack can be summed up thus.

- A decrease in the angle reduces lift and increases airspeed.

- An increase in the angle increases lift and decreases airspeed.

As the angle of attack is adjusted, with the corresponding changes in lift and airspeed, total drag (as depicted in Figure 3.23 on page 19) will vary.

Remember, Induced Drag is at its greatest at low speeds. Therefore the vortex effect is also at a maximum at low speeds.

The wake turbulence from vortex effect is thus going to be at its greatest during take-off and landing when angles of attack are high and speed is relatively low.

Wake turbulence is covered in the chapter on Meteorology (page 119) as it is very much influenced by atmospheric conditions.

Finally, increase the angle of attack too much and you will stall.

Stability

Why Stability?

By now you should be gaining a good working knowledge as to **why** your aircraft can fly – and more importantly, when it will cease to do so if you do not watch your airspeed.

Most of what has been discussed so far has assumed the aircraft to be in straight and level flight. However, just as a boat can be thrown around in rough sea conditions, so the same can happen to an aircraft in the rough flight conditions known as **turbulence**. To minimise the hard work that would face a pilot in countering this disturbance over a long in-flight period, modern aeroplanes have a built-in stability.

Taking first the case of turbulent air we are talking about those occasions when the aircraft can be dislodged or turned about in relation to its flight path by the air itself. The answer to this flight condition lies in the stability built into the aircraft.

What is Stability?

Stability is a condition which enables an aircraft to revert to its normal flight path without pilot input on those occasions when it is deflected from same.

To understand this means examining the different axes about which an aircraft can move (Figure 3.31 on page 24).

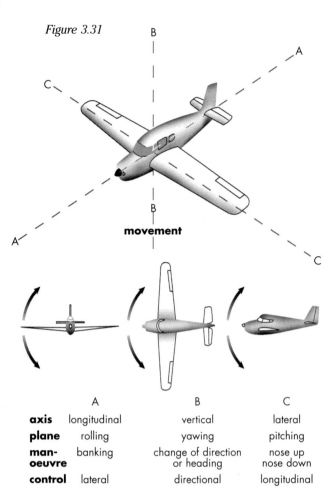

Figure 3.31

movement

	A	B	C
axis	longitudinal	vertical	lateral
plane	rolling	yawing	pitching
man-oeuvre	banking	change of direction or heading	nose up nose down
control	lateral	directional	longitudinal

Figure 3.31 introduces you to each axis about which an aeroplane can manoeuvre and the attitudes into which turbulence can 'throw' the machine out of straight and level. Later we will be discussing the controls which are used when an intended manoeuvre is required. In the meantime, back to built-in stability.

We will now look at the way in which stability is built in to cope with movements about each of the axes shown above.

Dihedral

Obtaining stability in the **Rolling Plane** is achieved by **Dihedral**. Looking at most aircraft head-on you will see that the tips of the wings are invariably higher than the roots. The angle thus subtended is known as the angle of dihedral (Figure 3.32).

Figure 3.32

In turbulent air a wing may drop (Figure 3.33).

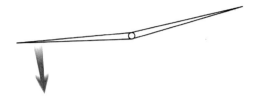

Figure 3.33

As the wing drops it will tend to slip in the direction of the drop. This creates a 'cross-wind' component in the airflow in relation to the wing (Figure 3.34).

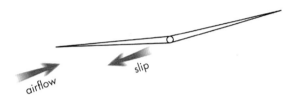

Figure 3.34

As the airflow meets the wing in this situation the lower wing meets the airflow at a greater angle of attack than the upper one and so provides increased lift, moving the wing back into level flight again (Figure 3.35).

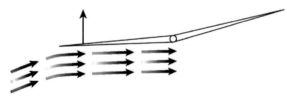

Figure 3.35

Stability in the Yawing Plane and Pitching Plane is normally obtained by fixed surfaces placed to the rear of the centre of gravity C of G although there are occasions when they will be found to the front of this point.

The surface acting in the yawing plane is called a **Fin** or **Keel**; the one acting in the pitching plane is known as a **Tailplane** (Figure 3.36 on page 25).

When the aircraft is dislodged from its intended flight path these fixed surfaces are presented to the airflow. The air is deflected and a force is set up at right angles to the deflected

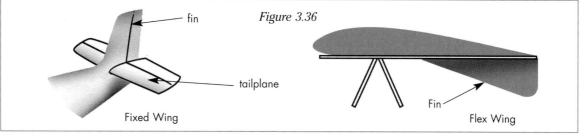

Figure 3.36

Fixed Wing

Flex Wing

air. This force moves the aircraft back into its original path (Figure 3.37).

Figure 3.37

Some microlights, for example the flexwing (weight shift) type, do not have a tailplane. (Do not imagine the word 'flexwing' means it is easy to roll up at the end of the day's flying! The word actually refers to the inherent flexibility of the wing in flight whereupon it gives way to an extent when hit by turbulent gusts. This relaxes the effect of the gusts and reduces the extent of the instability.) With these types of aircraft there is usually a marked degree of **Sweepback** on the wings. It is the area in proximity to each wing tip that acts as the fixed surface required aft of the C of G to give stability in the pitching plane. (Figure 3.38).

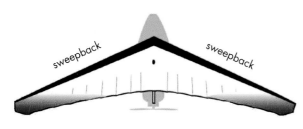

Figure 3.38

Others solve the pitch stability problem in trailing edges which are 'reflexed' so that in a dive the effect is to endeavour to restore level

flight. This reflex is usually to be found on the inboard halves of the wing (Figure 3.39).

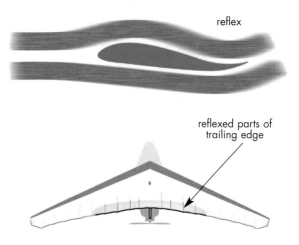

Figure 3.39

Centre of Pressure

Stability can also be influenced by variations in angle of attack. For simplicity sake lift has so far been depicted as a single force line acting at right angles to the airflow. In fact that single line represents the total lift generated which varies over the whole surface of the wing (Figure 3.40).

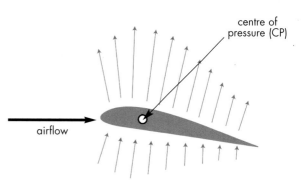

Figure 3.40

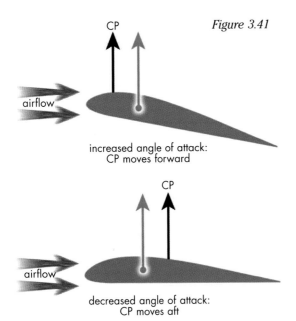

Figure 3.41

increased angle of attack:
CP moves forward

decreased angle of attack:
CP moves aft

The point on the aerofoil at which all the lift is said to act is known as the **Centre of Pressure** (CP) and it varies with the angle of attack.

An increase in this angle will see the centre of pressure move forward; a decrease will see it move aft (Figure 3.41 above).

Now look at what this can do to stability. (Figure 3.42).

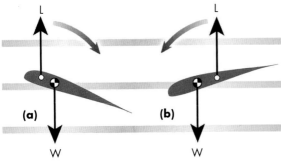

Figure 3.42

(a) increased angle of attack – forces out of balance
(b) decreased angle of attack – forces out of balance

So, apart from built-in stability being needed to combat turbulence, it is also needed to compensate for any movement of the centre of pressure.

A particular contribution to this stability is the tailplane on a fixed wing (three-axis) machine and the reflexed trailing edge on others.

Pendulum Effect

Finally, where stability is concerned, an important aspect is that of the pendulum effect on Weight force. The pendulum on a clock swings from side to side while the clock is ticking. But once the ticking stops the swinging eases off and the pendulum eventually stops at a point vertically below its pivot point on the clock above.

The weight on an aircraft, which is that of the aircraft itself, may not appear to swing like a pendulum but in turbulence it can roll to left or right or pitch up and down.

On a high-wing aeroplane the weight centre is well below the wing supporting it – similar to the pendulum being below the clock. Left to its own devices, should the wing drop to one side the weight will want to bring it back to level flight combined with the dihedral factor already discussed.

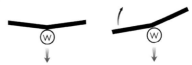

However, should the aeroplane be of the low-wing type the weight is virtually level with the wing so the weight influence is not so great. You will recall the reason for dihedral dealt with earlier, so a simple proof of the varying weight effect is visibly noticed by the degree of dihedral.

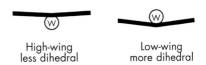

High-wing
less dihedral

Low-wing
more dihedral

When it comes to aircraft types such as the flex-wing and particularly the parachute, the effect is more positive. Both trike unit and parachutist are not rigidly fixed to the wing or canopy so the weight is more free to remain in the vertical as does the pendulum pivoted to a clock.

Control

Here we are going to be concerned with movement out of straight and level flight – the business of going where you want to go. This may be a climb, a descent, a turn, or maybe a combination of both turn and climb or descent.

Strictly speaking, how polished you will make the manoeuvres is a matter for your flying instructor to address; but how they take place and what is happening at the time does call for your becoming familiar with the control surfaces that enable the manoeuvre to take place.

Stability was achieved by *fixed* (fin and tailplane) surfaces, which when momentarily out of line with the airflow caused the aircraft to return to its original flight path. It will therefore come as no surprise to know that certainly in the case of **fixed wing (3-axis)** aeroplanes the manoeuvring is achieved by *movable* surfaces which are introduced into the airflow to set up forces that will deliberately cause a change in flight path. These movable surfaces are known as aerodynamic controls.

Such movable surface controls in the traditional sense do not apply to the flexwing (weightshift) type (often known as 'trikes' except for those that are foot-launched). Later it will be seen that in this case manoeuvres are by movement of the entire wing – combined with weightshift.

First we will cover the 3-axis control system, taking each manoeuvre in turn.

Fixed wing (3-axis) Control
Pitch
Pitch is the name given to the manoeuvre which produces a nose-up or nose-down attitude. As you saw earlier under the section on 'stability', it takes place about the lateral axis of the aeroplane.

The aerodynamic control is by means of movable surfaces called **elevators**, invariably attached to the rear of the tailplane (Figure 3.43).

There are aeroplanes with an all-moving tailplane which does the work of elevators

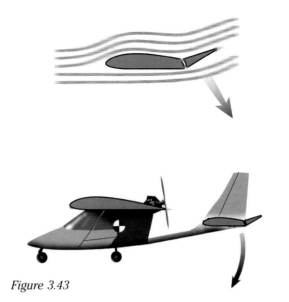

Figure 3.43

when moved up or down – cuts costs, I suppose!

In a nutshell: pitch down and airspeed increases with the decreased angle of attack. Pitch up and airspeed drops away as the angle of attack increases. There may be short-term changes in height by pitch control inputs such as a flare to temporarily reduce your rate of descent just prior to touch-down on landing.

Power
Although not specific to the issue of aerodynamic control, on the part of the 'car-minded' there can be the thought that speed in flight is controlled at all times by power. This is not so – you should take note of the fact that for long-term periods of changing height, **you increase power to *climb* and decrease power to *descend*.** (In case you see a glider *with no power* suddenly climb like a 'dingbat' after streaking across a gliding site, it will be due to the speed built up in a dive. In the absence of power the rate of climb in such an event immediately begins to fall away!)

The Turn
Roll
Roll is manoeuvring the aeroplane about its longitudinal axis in order to set up an angle of **bank**. You may recall when covering **'The Four Forces in Flight'** that it is the bank position that produces the force to set the turn in motion due to the horizontal component of

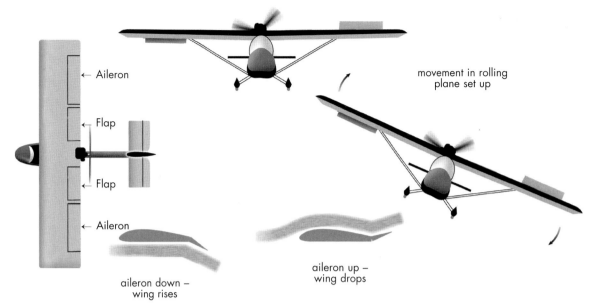

Figure 3.44

the lift force. At first you may think that it is the rudder that performs the turn, as it does on a boat; this is not the case, but more later.

We can induce roll by aerodynamic control in the form of **ailerons**. These are movable surfaces attached to the trailing edge at the end of each wing (Figure 3.44).

The aileron, when in the **down** position, alters the shape of the wing in that it **increases** the angle of attack and the wing rises due to the increased lift. Conversely, the aileron in the **up** position at the same time **decreases** the angle of attack with the decrease in lift causing it to descend. The result is a roll towards the required angle of bank for the desired rate of turn.

Returning to the state of forces in the bank, you will recall that the vertical component of the lift force is no longer equal to the weight; the result could be the nose beginning to drop in the turn.

This is prevented by an input of pitch-up control which increases the angle of attack and provides additional lift to match the weight and maintain level flight in the turn (Figure 3.45). There is one point to remember: an increase in angle of attack means a decrease in airspeed; ensure that it is adequate in the

turn so that this decrease does not take you below stall speed.

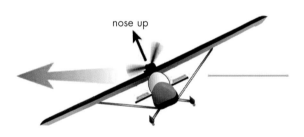

Figure 3.45

As an aside, ailerons are particularly useful in that they are able to keep the wing down when taxiing, taking off and landing in an element of crosswind.

While on the aileron theme, there is another form of roll control in the form of a movable surface known as **spoilers**. Placed on both wings at the point of maximum lift, when one is deployed the lift is reduced in the immediate vicinity by the destruction of a previously smooth airflow. The result is a roll towards the descending (inner) wing (Figure 3.46 on page 29).

Flaps are covered later on page 31.

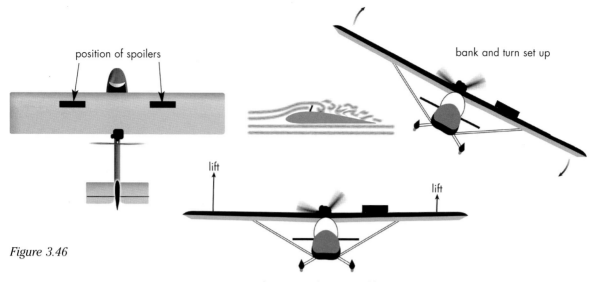

Figure 3.46

spoiler activated – uneven lift set up

Yaw

Yaw is said to take place when the aeroplane slips inwards or skids outwards away from the path (direction) in which it is intended to travel.

As mentioned earlier, the rudder is often mistaken by the uninitiated as being the correct means of achieving a turn in an aeroplane, similar to applying the steering wheel in a car.

When a car goes into a turn it normally ends up travelling in the direction it is pointing. However, should the road be covered in a sheet of ice, the car can turn towards its desired direction but due to the ice it will continue to skid along its original path.

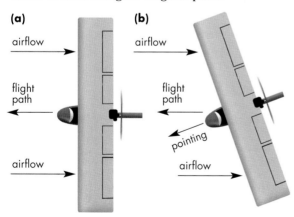

Figure 3.47 (a) Flight path in line with pointing (b) Original flight path and new pointing diverge; yaw is set up

An aeroplane travelling through the air is constantly 'on ice' in the sense that when wanting to change direction it has no road on which the tyres can grip to ensure the change will take place. Attempting to turn by rudder will result in a 'skid' along its existing path – at least initially (Figure 3.47).

We will now look at some other occasions when skid/slip occurs through the use of rudder.

Yaw has a further effect in that it can induce a roll. With an input of rudder, the aeroplane may initially skid outwards but as the aeroplane moves around its vertical axis, the outer wing will move faster than the inner wing.

The faster wing will therefore produce more lift and rise with the inner wing descending as it undergoes a decrease in lift from its slower airspeed. The outcome is the aeroplane starting to roll into the turn, due to what is termed **the further effect of yaw** (Figure 3.48 on page 30).

The further effect of yaw may be accentuated due to the effect of dihedral. The sideways airflow induced by the skid combines with the dihedral of the outer wing to increase lift (Figure 3.49 on page 30).

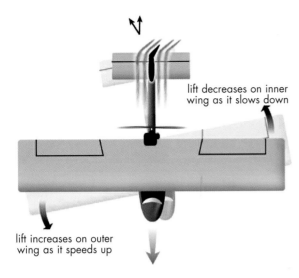

lift decreases on inner
wing as it slows down

lift increases on outer
wing as it speeds up

Figure 3.48 Wing pivots about vertical axis; aircraft yaws to left; rolling movement is set up

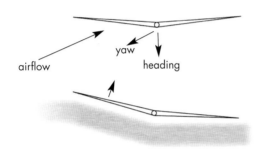

airflow

yaw

heading

Figure 3.49 Yaw sets up a sideways move or 'skid'. Dihedral angle becomes an angle of attack. Additional lift results on outer wing – assisting the rolling movement.

Any 2-axis aeroplane (devoid of ailerons) has no alternative but to turn by the use of rudder to initiate roll for a desired bank.

Yaw can also be produced when the down-going aileron increases the angle of attack on the outer wing and creates increased induced drag. This causes the wing to yaw round in the opposite way to the intended turn.

This effect is known as **adverse yaw** and is countered by the input of rudder; this effect can be reduced by fitting differential ailerons. Here the arc of the down-going aileron is reduced compared with the arc of the up-going one, thus ensuring that the drag on the lower wing is greater than that on the upper wing (Figure 3.50).

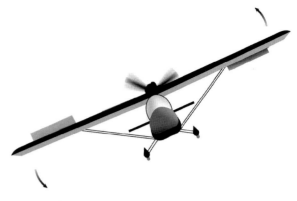

Figure 3.50

Finally, in a roll manoeuvre only, the aeroplane may slip inwards, and this roll can be accentuated by the fin/rudder combination acting as a 'weathercock' – the result is a nose drop.

We can now see that turns may be initiated by the use of aileron or rudder. At low airspeeds, when adverse yaw may be an issue, initiating the turn with rudder will assist the ailerons in executing a turn. Of course, 2-axis aeroplanes have no choice and must rely on the rudder alone.

The Balanced Turn

A balanced turn is one where the aeroplane is turning at the correct angle of bank for the desired rate of turn, at constant speed with no skid or slip. As mentioned earlier, for any nose drop for whatever reason during a turn, the matter is corrected by a pitch-up input to increase the angle of attack.

There is an instrument called the **balance ball** which will tell you when you are on the right path (Figure 3.51). Should you not have one, but happen to be in an open cockpit, the airflow can give you a good indication.

Figure 3.51

On a turn to the left, if you feel the airflow on your right cheek then you are skidding out to the right; if on the left cheek, you are slipping to the left. When it blows straight into your face you have got your act together!

If you happen to be in a closed cockpit, many pilots use a good wrinkle: they fix a **streamer** of wool or ribbon in front of them on the fuselage or windscreen. Only when the streamer is pointing directly at you is a balanced turn being made (Figure 3.52).

Figure 3.52

The art of exercising a balanced turn can require a combination of all forms of control being used at the same time. It is an art which must be confined to the tuition your instructor will provide.

Ancillary Controls on a 3-axis Aeroplane

Apart from controls directly associated with manoeuvres there are other controls available which all contribute to easier and safer flight. They are flaps, slats, trim tabs, balance tabs, balance and air brakes.

Flaps

The safest landing is the one which can be made at the minimum of airspeed with the minimum of landing run. At present you may consider that this is the very area in which the microlight scores; but with some now bordering on the performance of light aeroplanes the problem cannot be ignored.

Maximum lift for minimum airspeed can be obtained from a 'nice fat aerofoil' with plenty of top camber. However, the form drag such a shape would produce precludes any decent cruise speed.

The answer lies in altering the wing shape to produce lift at low speed when the occasion warrants it. This facility is brought about by the use of flaps.

Flaps are movable surfaces which extend downwards into the airflow. They are to be found at the trailing edge of each wing between the root and the aileron.

Although there are different types of flaps (Figure 3.53 below) they all basically serve the same purpose – to increase lift and drag at low speed.

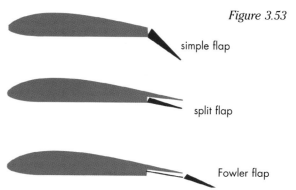

Figure 3.53

simple flap

split flap

Fowler flap

When a flap is deployed note how the airflow reacts. Not only does the camber increase – together with a wing area increase in the case of the Fowler flap – but the obstruction in the airflow creates a 'warning' to the air ahead. There is an increase in the airflow going over the top of the wing and the speeding up this undergoes adds to lift already produced by camber (Figure 3.54 below).

The angle to which a flap is deployed is very important.

Small Angle	– Small increase in drag
	– Large increase in lift
Large Angle	– Large increase in drag
	– Little further increase in lift

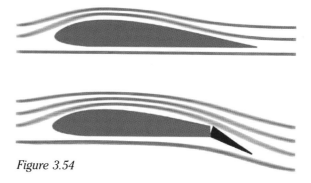

Figure 3.54

Hence you have small angles of flap associated with take-off and large angles in the landing configuration.

Slats

Another way of increasing lift at low speed is to delay the stall beyond the point at which it would normally happen; to permit a greater angle of attack, and thereby a lower airspeed, without lift breaking down.

This situation can be achieved by channelling the airflow through a gap at the leading edge of the wing which speeds up that flow and thus increases lift (Venturi effect). Also, by virtue of the angle at which it is directed on to the wing, there is a delay in the breakdown of the smooth airflow (Figure 3.55).

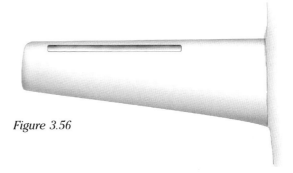

Figure 3.56

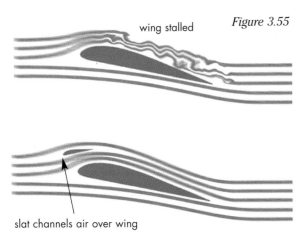

wing stalled   *Figure 3.55*

slat channels air over wing

The device which enables all this to take place is known as a **slat** and the gap it forms is known as a **slot**.

Slats are fixed or movable surfaces found at the leading edge of the wing and are aerofoil in shape. The movable type are usually flush with the leading edge and they are 'sucked' out into the airflow as the airspeed slackens off with the increase in angle of attack which in turn causes the reduction in pressure to allow this to happen.

Sometimes the gap or slot is built into the leading edge of the wing as opposed to being a separate surface. Such a wing is called a **slotted wing** (Figure 3.56).

Trim Tabs

Should a control surface have to be deployed into the airflow for any length of time the resistance met can prove tiring for the pilot.

The problem is overcome by the use of trim tabs. These are small movable surfaces set in the trailing edge of the main control surfaces (Figure 3.57).

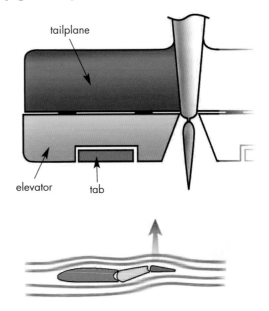

tailplane

elevator   tab

Figure 3.57

If maintaining pitch-up control is becoming tedious the tab is deployed in the opposite direction to the control surface and the air thus deflected exerts a force upwards on the elevator thus easing or removing any effort to maintain the elevator in an up position.

Ground adjustable **fixed trim tabs** are sometimes fitted to an aileron or rudder to allow for the making of initial flight test adjustments.

Balance

Purely from an interest point of view and in order to avoid confusion should you ever hear the name there is also another tab called a **balance tab**.

Control input on a very large aircraft can take quite an amount of strength due to the weight and size of the surfaces. Identical in looks and position with a trim tab, the balance tab however cannot be moved at will by the pilot. It is fixed so that it will go the opposite way to the control surfaces at all times, thus assisting the pilot to move the controls. More often than not you will see the two side by side (Figure 3.58(a)).

(a)

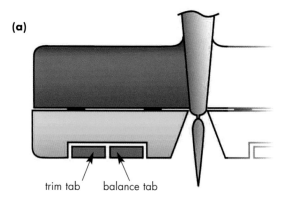

trim tab   balance tab

(b)

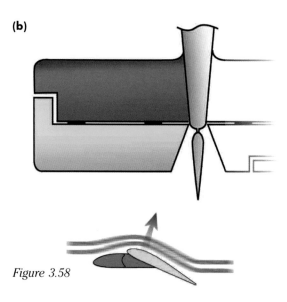

Figure 3.58

Figure 3.58(b) shows another method of achieving help in moving heavy controls by means known as a graduated balance or shielded

horn control surface hinged so that an inset segment protrudes into the airflow which in turn pushes that surface in the direction intended.

A final variation to the theme is the **anti-balance tab**. Large control surfaces may not produce sufficient force feedback to the pilot; the all-moving tailplane referred to on page 27 is an example. If a tab is arranged to move in the same direction to the control surface it will provide a restoring force and tend to return it to the neutral position.

Air Brakes

The need can arise to slow down and lose height rapidly – maybe to land in the only available field in the vicinity due to an engine failure.

Air Brakes enable one to do just this. They are flat plates inset into the wing about one-third of the chord from the leading edge. When deployed they project up into the airflow and the disturbance they cause destroys lift in their vicinity. Air brakes can be single or in pairs. Single brakes are found only on the upper surface; doubles appearing above and below (Figure 3.59).

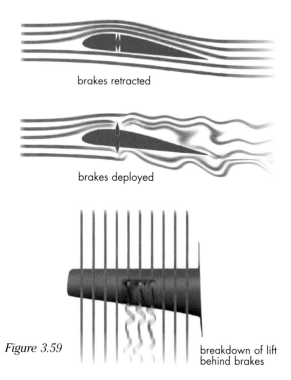

brakes retracted

brakes deployed

Figure 3.59

breakdown of lift behind brakes

You will recall an earlier mention of spoilers which are used in place of ailerons (Spoilerons) when deployed singly on one wing or another to initiate bank. When both spoilers are deployed simultaneously they naturally take on the role of air brakes.

Flexwing (Weight Shift) Control

Here we have a situation where there are no aerodynamic controls. Attached to the wing in front of the pilot is the control frame, a triangle of tubing sometimes referred to as an 'A' frame. It is the means by which you control all manoeuvres.

The control frame is fixed to the wing, and the tube at the bottom of the triangle, called the **control bar**, is the one you normally handle. On the ground you can effortlessly move the wing in any direction using the control bar, but in flight the situation is slightly different (Figure 3.60(a)).

The inherent stability of the wing in flight produces an element of rigidity compared to the trike unit. This allows you, when pushing or pulling the bar, not only to move the wing slightly, but also to dislodge the trike unit (pendulum weight) from equilibrium. This is because you are pushing or pulling against a part of the aeroplane that in a sense wants to remain steady (Figure 3.60(b)).

The subtle flexing and changing shape of the wing, touched upon earlier when discussing 'Stability', is an extremely complex process. Some of the features you will see incorporated into it are virtually an attempt to mirror the almost infinite subtleties of a bird's wing!

Pitch

Quite simply, the control bar is pulled back to decrease the angle of attack and increase speed; it is pushed forward to increase the angle of attack and decrease speed (Figure 3.61).

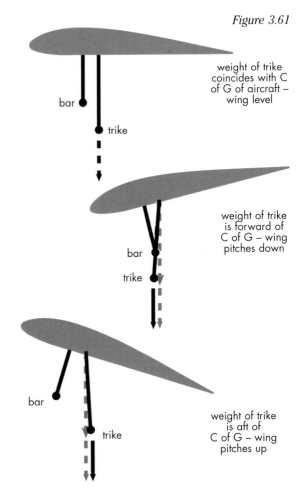

Figure 3.61

weight of trike coincides with C of G of aircraft – wing level

weight of trike is forward of C of G – wing pitches down

weight of trike is aft of C of G – wing pitches up

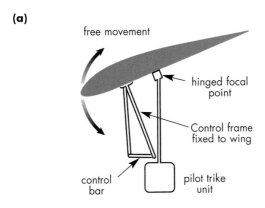

(a)

free movement

hinged focal point

Control frame fixed to wing

control bar

pilot trike unit

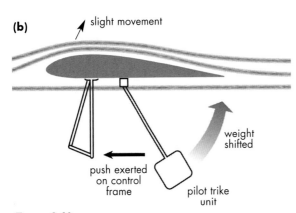

(b)

slight movement

weight shifted

push exerted on control frame

pilot trike unit

Figure 3.60

Some flexwing aircraft are equipped with a pitch trim system. This allows the pilot to fly at a higher cruise speed without the need to constantly pull back on the control bar. The trim system may allow the pilot to optimise the shape of the wing for the cruise whilst in flight. Alternatively, an electric actuator in the trike may apply a force directly to the wing to reduce the control load.

The Turn
Roll

As is the case with the 3-axis aeroplanes, a turn in a flexwing is created by inducing **roll** to set up the desired bank to produce that horizontal inward force.

To roll to the left the control bar is moved to the right. Initially, the trike/pilot unit (or pilot only) will move out of equilibrium to the left; the wing will also roll slightly to the left due to the bar input (Figure 3.62).

(a)

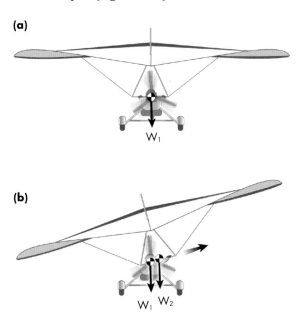

(b)

Figure 3.62 (a) Level flight (b) Bar moved to right; weight shifts to left; roll is set up.

However, as the above movement of the wing takes place, there is another movement which immediately sets the full roll in motion. In all trikes there is flexibility built into the wing (sail) which allows it to change its shape at the time the weight redistribution takes place.

The process is known as **billow shift**, which allows the inner wing in the turn to slacken and 'balloon' out slightly while the outer wing becomes more taut.

Various mechanisms and features are incorporated into the design of the flexwing to achieve billow shift; the principal mechanism utilised in current designs is the **floating cross tube** (Figure 3.63).

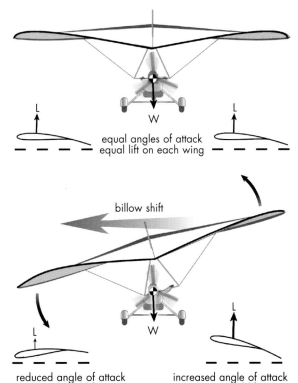

Figure 3.63

The roll sequence on, say, a left turn would be thus:

– on pushing the control bar to the right the weight of the trike unit is shifted to the left towards the inner wing

– initial roll to the left takes place due to this 'shift' of the trike weight which increases the load on the inner wing

– the additional load draws the keel to the left which tightens the outer (right) wing and slackens the inner (left) wing

– the tightness on the outer wing draws down the trailing edge which increases the angle of attack, and with it comes an increase in lift

- the slackness on the inner wing lets it 'billow out', the trailing edge rises and the angle of attack decreases, bringing about a decrease in lift

The result is a roll about the longitudinal axis.

Yaw

There is no rudder to induce an outward skid on a flexwing, but as the roll commences a slip towards the inner wing can be induced. When this happens a sideways component of the airflow is such that there is more form drag over the wing to the rear of the C of G than there is at the front of it. The result is the wing beginning to turn inwards and the nose to drop (Figure 3.64).

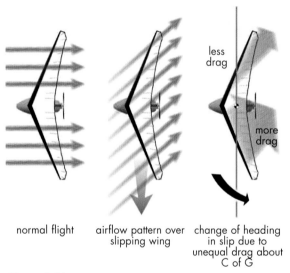

less drag

more drag

normal flight   airflow pattern over slipping wing   change of heading in slip due to unequal drag about C of G

Figure 3.64

Some flexwing microlights have a vertical fin above or below the rear of the wing, aft of the C of G. As the wing slips in the roll a 'weathercock' situation adds a contribution to the inwards turn and nose-drop in a similar manner to the fin/rudder combination on a 3-axis aeroplane.

The Balanced Turn

As with the 3-axis aeroplanes, the balanced turn will be the setting up of the correct angle of bank for the desired rate of turn at a constant airspeed. In this case there would be no skid problem to face but the possibility of a

slip is rectified, or better still prevented from the outset, by the appropriate pitch-up input.

The Powered Parachute

The powered parachute is provided with a trike unit with a canopy instead of a wing. It has no form of pitch control; it relies on power to climb and a decrease in power to descend. Perhaps the best approach to dealing with this type of aeroplane is to look at the nature of the **paraglider** and forget the power element for the moment.

A paraglider wing is primarily controlled by changing the shape of the trailing edge through the use of **Control Lines** attached to **Control Handles** situated to the left and right of the canopy. When the handles are left alone the canopy will be in a fully up position; when pulled down the trailing edge of the canopy will be lowered into a **'lip'** (Figure 3.65).

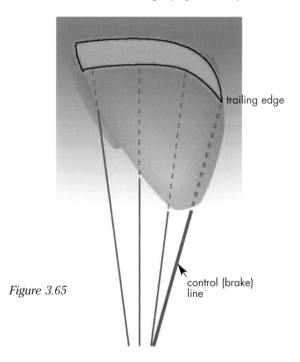

trailing edge

Figure 3.65

control (brake) line

Pitch

When the 'lip' is in position after both control lines have been applied at the same time, then both drag and lift will be increased. The drag will be substantial and produce a rapid and large decrease in airspeed. The increase in the angle of attack induced by the formation of the 'lip' will produce a modest increase of lift.

Some aircraft of this type are fitted with a pitch trim system which allows the angle of the canopy to be adjusted in flight in relation to the aircraft's longitudinal datum line as opposed to the angle of attack (Figure 3.66). This can increase or decrease the airspeed, which would otherwise be fixed in level flight.

The Turn
Yaw

When a single control is applied, say the left-hand one, the left half of the canopy span will be pulled down forming a defined 'lip' which creates increased drag. The extra drag on the left will cause the canopy to yaw to the left (Figure 3.67).

Roll

The further effect of yaw will now induce the secondary effect of less lift on the left and increased lift on the right of the canopy, thus wanting the aircraft to roll and turn to the left. The roll created will overcome any lift induced at the left-hand side on the lowering of the canopy.

Power Input

It was said earlier that the powered parachute had no formal pitch control – it ascended by an increase in power and descended by a

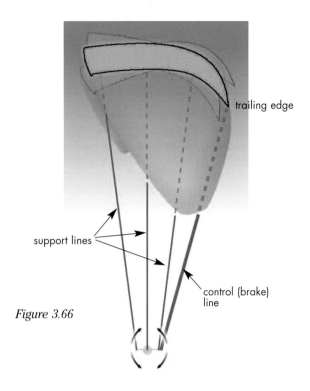

trailing edge

support lines

control (brake) line

Figure 3.66

reduction. The result of this means that it is confined to a fixed airspeed when in level flight.

Of course, should this aircraft be fitted with a pitch trim system then variations of airspeed in level flight are possible. One reason that airspeed in level flight for a given aircraft will vary is the weight of the pilot: a heavier pilot will require more airspeed; this in turn will require more power to secure the additional lift needed to maintain a constant height, with yet additional power required to achieve an ascent.

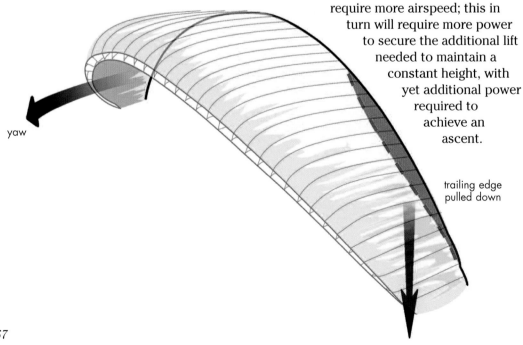

yaw

trailing edge pulled down

Figure 3.67

The *Microlight Pilot's Handbook* is geared to taking a student through the areas required for passing the examination in order to attain the National Private Pilots Licence (Microlight) – NPPL(M).

The following text is confined to areas where no licence is required and therefore no examination is involved, and also to areas related to older machines in which initial training is no longer likely to take place, but you might just buy such a machine in the future.

Unlicensed Aircraft
Foot Launched Microlights
The official term for a Foot Launched Microlight (FLM) is a Self-Propelled Hang Glider (SPHG). These terms, however, are potentially misleading as a FLM may be equipped with wheels and a SPHG may be a paramotor (back-pack powered parachute)! The technical definition of a SPHG may be found on page 91.

The Paramotor
The control system already covered in respect of the powered parachute applies in many ways to the paramotor.

Perhaps it is as well to emphasise the correct use of both toggles at the same time for a reduction of speed on landing – most important for the protection of the human undercarriage: the pilot's legs!

There are no doubt other factors contributing to the main control system with which your instructor will familiarise you. If you are sufficiently insane to enter this aspect of microlight flying without an instructor at the outset then you would not be reading this book anyway!

The Powered Hang Glider
The powered hang glider is known as the forerunner of flexwing microlights as far as the UK is concerned. Relatively recently it has been re-born, appropriately into the FLM category.

All the controls will be the same as the 'trike', but this time in the absence of a trike unit the movement of the pilot's body alone induces the necessary weight shift, as in the unpowered hang glider.

Other Forms of Control
As a matter of interest, you may come across types of microlight which have other forms of aerodynamic control than those we have already covered.

Turn
Some are fitted with vertical movable surfaces at the extremity of the wings; they are known as tip draggers and act independently of each other. Their effect is best described using a water analogy.

If you are under way in a rowing boat with the oars shipped (to the non-sailor, this means out of the water!) and you place one oar in the briny the boat will at once turn in the direction of the immersed oar. The oar has caused drag and the boat has pivoted about that drag point (the oar) (Figure 3.68).

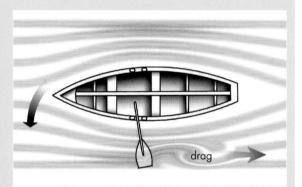

Figure 3.68

By now you should be able to deduce what will happen when a dragger is deployed. The drag causes induced yaw with the further effect being bank (Figure 3.69).

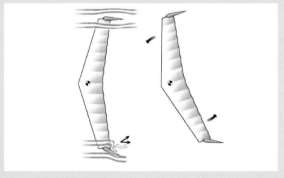

Figure 3.69 Left dragger induces drag. An example of this format is the Pterodactyl.

Pitch

Early versions of the Pterodactyl also rely on weight shift for pitching, but on this occasion the shift is made by the pilot moving part of his/her body or simply leaning forwards or backwards in the hammock-type seat (Figure 3.70).

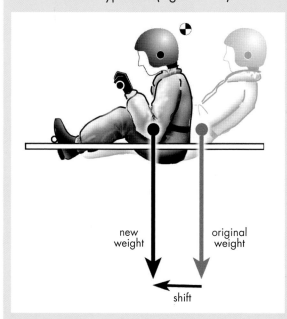

Figure 3.70

There are a few light aeroplane types which have their elevators attached to a form of tail-plane fitted at the front; in this case the fixed surface is called a canard. (Please do not ask where this name came from – I shall 'duck' from making any answer!)

Sometimes a fixed canard is designed as a miniature wing with lift-creating capability and is set at an angle of incidence greater than the main wing. This means that should the aero-plane pitch up too steeply the canard will stall first, causing the nose to drop and avoiding the main wing stalling at all.

An example of this type of microlight is the Eagle – reputed to be the safest aeroplane in the world because of this stall prevention. The Eagle's elevators on its canard are attached by lines to the pilot's swinging seat (Figure 3.71).

Their operation is then made possible by the pilot initiating a backward movement in the seat for pitch up and forwards for pitch down. These seat movements for elevator control are also a form of weight shift.

A surface at the front can also be of the all-flying format. The later versions of Pterodactyl were fitted thus to do away with the body movement weight-shift method for pitch control mentioned previously (Figure 3.72).

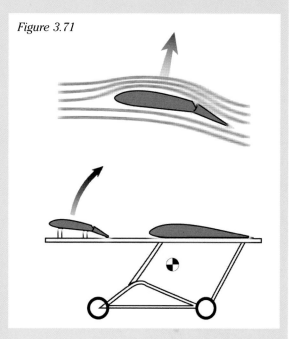

Figure 3.71

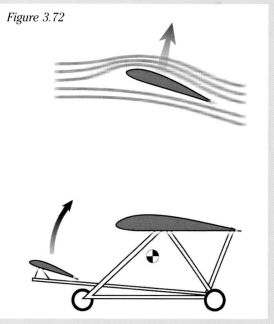

Figure 3.72

Forces at Play

Forces related to flight have already been touched upon at the outset when such areas as lift/weight and thrust/drag were discussed. Apart from the control you can exercise as a pilot, there are forces that can be created which also have an input of which you should be aware.

Thrust

But first let us take the ideal situation. When in straight and level flight at a constant airspeed the forces balance out by equalling each other: thrust equals drag and lift equal weight.

Some people think that thrust (power) must always exceed the drag or the aeroplane will stay still – it only does so when the aircraft is accelerating. However, drag also increases with airspeed and there comes a point when the power can no longer accelerate any more and speed becomes constant. Drag has finally equalled thrust.

An aeroplane is able to climb as long as 'excess' power is available. On reaching your selected height, if you maintain that height the lift equals weight. Reduce power too much and you will descend. Remember, power controls ascent and descent; also, less lift is produced in a climb than in a descent.

So, in straight and level flight at constant speed the opposing forces balance each other out (Figure 3.73) and the aircraft is said to be in equilibrium.

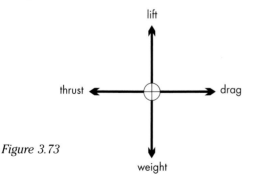

Figure 3.73

Weight shift as a control element has already been covered; but there are occasions when weight (such as luggage) is improperly stored to the extent that the aeroplane's C of G is badly out of place.

The result can be a nose-down or nose-up situation, which you would constantly have to overcome by pitch control to maintain level flight; this can be a strenuous call on the muscles! (Figure 3.74)

The movement of the aeroplane's C of G may also very the pitch stability experienced by the pilot. When the C of G is moved forward the pitch stability will increase and, conversely, when the C of G is moved aft then pitch stability will reduce.

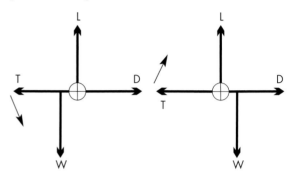

Figure 3.74

Thrust Line

Pitch control can also be affected by a variety of events. It can be due to the thrust line (the positioning of the engine could be out of tune related to the drag line). There can be turning effects when the propeller torque changes with power and even when the slipstream alters from its norm.

Invariably the design of the aeroplane takes this into account for cruise speed, but it can have an adverse effect with sudden power increases or decreases causing a sudden pitch up or down – particularly near the ground.

For example, think of a powered back-pack

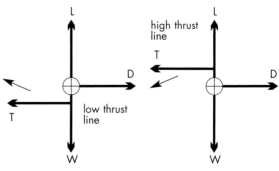

Figure 3.75

Figure 3.76

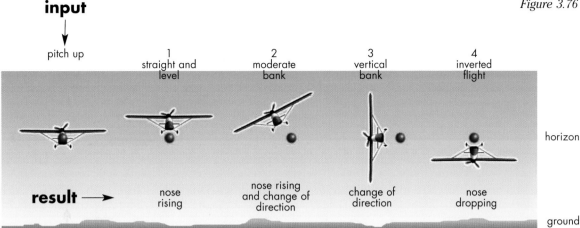

input

↓

pitch up

| 1 straight and level | 2 moderate bank | 3 vertical bank | 4 inverted flight |

result →

nose rising | nose rising and change of direction | change of direction | nose dropping

horizon

ground

parachute about to land. A sudden burst of power here could make the pilot/engine unit dart temporarily forward and eventually begin to oscillate at just the wrong time (Figure 3.75).

Manoeuvres out of Straight and Level

So far the effect of controls has been discussed taking each control in isolation and assuming application is being made from the stable state of straight and level flight.

What if the same inputs are made when out of straight and level?

The situation is best grasped by understanding that in whatever attitude your aeroplane finds itself, the input of a particular control will have the same effect on it as in level flight.

That is, the movement will still be in relation to the appropriate axis of the aeroplane. However, the movement might be far from the same in relation to the horizon or the ground.

The effect is best shown visually. (Figure 3.76 above).

Notice how in attitude 2 the use of pitch up has not only raised the nose but has caused a change in direction. In attitude 3 it is acting totally as a rudder whilst in 4 the outcome is the nose dropping.

Take a small model of an aeroplane and demonstrate to yourself the movements it should make as you apply imaginary control inputs of not only pitch but yaw and roll also – all with the model in various attitudes.

Turning

The most frequent manoeuvre you will make is a turn. Earlier it was said that in flying it needed a blend of two manoeuvres at the same time to execute a turn – a combination of roll and yaw. In fact pitch plays a part as well.

You have already learned that the input of yaw on its own results in a change of heading with the aeroplane itself tending to skid along its original path – flying off at a tangent you might say.

Inducing your machine to prescribe a circle needs the input of a force acting towards the centre of that circle – as if the aeroplane is tethered to a pole and forced to fly round it.

The force used to do just this is lift. As roll is induced and the wing is banked – note the disposition of the forces in the resulting parallelogram of forces (Figure 3.77).

Figure 3.77

Figure 3.78

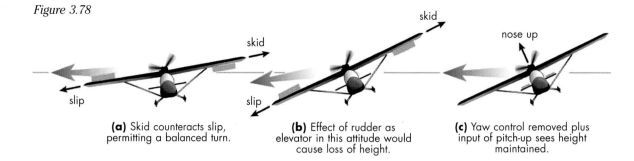

(a) Skid counteracts slip, permitting a balanced turn.

(b) Effect of rudder as elevator in this attitude would cause loss of height.

(c) Yaw control removed plus input of pitch-up sees height maintained.

You can see how lift divides into two other forces – one acting vertically and the other an inwards force pulling the aeroplane towards the centre of the turn. This force is known as **Centripetal Force** (CF); forget for a moment the fact that V is now less than L – more on this later.

However, induce roll on its own and the ensuing slip will cause a loss in height.

An input of just the right amount of yaw sorts this out as the resulting skid counteracts the slip – demonstrating the simultaneous combination of roll and yaw needed to initiate a balanced turn.

As the turn develops, the rudder will begin to act as an elevator due to the attitude of the aeroplane and once again height could be lost; also the outer wing travels faster than the inner one in a turn so the increased lift on the outer wing could induce more roll than required.

Both these possibilities are checked by an input of pitch-up control, at the same time taking off yaw and any tendency towards too much roll is countered by easing of roll input (Figure 3.78).

To achieve a very tight turn – one of small radius – means increasing bank so that CF is increased in order to achieve this aim (Figure 3.79).

However, increasing CF results in a further decrease in force V which acts vertically to support weight (W). Again, the problem this can cause and how to avoid it will be discussed later.

The Trike in a Turn

The question must be going through your mind as to where the Trike figures in all this. After all there are no rudder or draggers to provide that initial yaw to balance the turn.

In fact the trike cannot yaw in the conventional sense but in turning overall it does have other facets which play a part.

Turning a trike starts with inducing bank and setting up centripetal force in the same way as just discussed. As bank occurs, slip results and the situation is as shown in Figure 3.64 on page 36.

In Figure 3.64, the form drag will be greater aft of the C of G due to there being more sail area in this sector. The varying drag values induce a change of heading without the need for a movable surface such as a rudder.

Also, some trikes have a vertical fin keel surface above or below the wing aft of the C of G. (Figure 3.80).

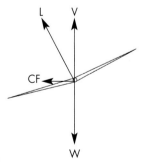

Figure 3.79

Figure 3.80

CHAPTER 3

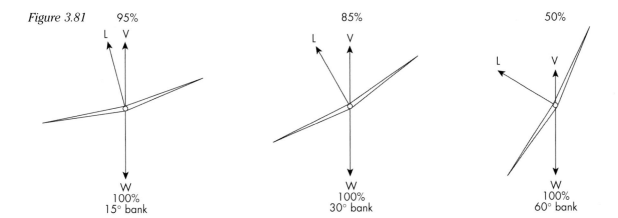

Figure 3.81

95%	85%	50%
W 100% 15° bank	W 100% 30° bank	W 100% 60° bank

As bank is induced a 'weathercock' effect assists a change of direction as the wing slips.

Once again the obvious loss of height that will come about by slip through roll input alone is countered with a pitch-up input by pushing out the bar.

At this point it might not be amiss to mention that pilots accustomed to a 3-axis control system – the name given to control by rudder, elevator and ailerons – may find their initial handling of a trike a most stimulating experience!

This is because the control movement with the bar will be opposite to what has probably become instinctive.

Suffice it to say, this is not the problem many think it to be. Countless pilots fly both types without thinking about it – simply because they underwent conversion tuition with a good trike instructor who understood their needs.

The Balanced Turn

Finally, how can you tell if your turn is balanced? There are instruments available but if you, or just your head, is out in the open there is no need for them.

Suppose you enter a left hand turn. Too much roll input and as you slip, the airstream will strike the left hand side of your face. Too much yaw and as you skid the right hand side will feel the breeze.

You have 'got it together' when the air is striking you full in the face.

Pilots flying under cover often fix a streamer of, say, wool or ribbon outside the cockpit directly in front of them. Movement of the streamer to one side or the other will indicate slip or skid. When it is straight in line – all is well. (See Figure 3.52 on page 31.)

Airspeed in a Turn

Yes, you have come across the term 'turn' before, but there are some aspects that have yet to be covered now that you have absorbed the basics. You may come across some repetition, but it does no harm to recap occasionally!

Stalling Speed in a Turn

This aspect of airspeed in the turn is rather complicated but every effort will be made to keep the explanation as simple as possible.

Refer back to Figure 3.79 (page 42) for a moment. As CP increases in a bank, so there comes about an inevitable decrease in the vertical component (V) which supports weight (W).

If no steps are taken to counter this decrease then the result will be a descending turn.

In a bank the rate at which V drops below W is minimal at first but it becomes very marked as the bank increases and likewise does the rate of descent.

The extent to which this happens is shown by equating V as a percentage of W in varying angles of bank (Figure 3.81 above).

It should now be obvious that to execute a balanced turn with no loss of height it is crucial that V remains equal to W. This can only

Figure 3.82

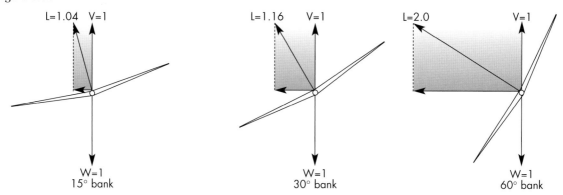

be achieved by increasing the angle of attack, thus increasing lift (L) and thereby increasing V until it is equal to W.

However, on increasing the angle of attack there will be an increase in induced drag and a decrease in airspeed. This calls for a gradual increase in power as the turn progresses so that adequate airspeed is maintained.

It is crucial to be aware of just what is an adequate airspeed in a turn. The question needs further examination as the stalling speed also increases in this manoeuvre.

The question by how much is a different matter if a precise explanation is to be given.

First we take a look at by how much L must be increased to ensure V equals W as bank steepens. Refer to the parallelogram of forces in Figure 3.82.

In each of the above angles of bank the value of L can be ascertained by measuring the diagonal L against the vertical side V. Without being ultra-accurate (by using Pythagorus) you will see that given L = 1 in level flight then for V to = 1:

at 15° of bank → L required = × 1.04

at 30° of bank → L required = × 1.16

at 60° of bank → L required = × 2.00

If you have to produce twice the lift to maintain height in a turn at 60° of bank then it means a substantial increase in angle of attack will be required and consequently a substantial increase in power to maintain an adequate airspeed.

It will also mean a substantial increase in your stalling speed at this angle.

Concerning the increase in stalling speed in a turn referred to earlier it will be imperceptible at first but it goes up rapidly as you steepen the bank until almost 1.5 times normal at 60° of bank. So, if your stalling speed in level flight is say 30 mph then it can be around 45 mph in a 60° banking turn.

If you are interested in how this deduction is arrived at you must recall the speed squared law referred to earlier: Lift increases at the square of the speed.

In other words, if your speed goes up by ×2 then lift goes up by ×4 (2×2). For the issue under discussion look at this law in reverse. If the increase in lift required is ×4 then the airspeed required to produce that lift must increase by ×√4 which is ×2.

So, if the minimum speed for level flight is 30 mph then to produce ×4 lift the airspeed must be 30×2 which = 60 mph.

Suppose 30 mph happens to be the stalling speed, then in this situation the stalling speed will be 60 mph.

Apply this reasoning to the examples shown above after Figure 3.81 – taking 30 mph as the stalling speed.

To sum up, it is most important that you remember this: airspeed in any form of turn be it level, climbing or descending, must be sufficient to preclude a stall; hence the need for adequate power during such manoeuvres.

High-Speed Stall

You will remember that when yaw was set up there was a moment when the aircraft was heading in the new direction but actually travelling along the original path.

The same sort of situation can arise in the use of pitch control but with much more dire effect if you have insufficient height.

You are diving at a fairly high speed and suddenly decide to pitch the nose up. The nose will certainly go up but for a time the aircraft will continue on its downward path resulting in a sharp increase in the angle of attack.

If the stalling angle is exceeded then the smooth airflow over the wing will break away and a stall will take place even though your airspeed may be well above stalling speed as you know it.

You will have been subjected to what is known as a **High Speed Stall** and this condition is far from clever close to the ground. However,

with the low wing loading normally associated with microlights there should not be a problem with this type of aeroplane.

The Spin Off a Turn

First there is the effect from inducing yaw – carrying out a flat turn as it is called. You will recall how yaw causes a change of heading which slows down the inner wing whilst speeding up the outer one.

Now suppose your stalling speed is 30 mph and you enter a flat turn – or even unintentionally apply rudder – close to that speed. Should you do so at say 32 mph; the outer wing could well speed up to 36 mph and the inner wing slow down to 28 mph. At this speed the inner wing will stall and drop whilst the outer wing continues to produce lift. This can cause the aeroplane to flick over and enter a spiral descent about its vertical axis.

Similarly, if your wings are not level at the point of stall, the wing going down will meet the airflow at a greater angle of attack and stall with the other wing still producing lift.

Either way you end up in what is known as a **spin** (Figure 3.83).

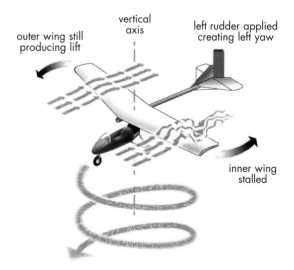

Figure 3.83

A spin must not be confused with a spiral dive. In a spin there is no increase in airspeed but vertical descent is very rapid.

In a spiral dive the aeroplane is not in a stalled condition. The nose is at a much steeper angle and the speed progressively builds up until it can reach dangerous levels. Any attempt to raise the nose would steepen the turn, so it is necessary to reduce the roll before easing out of the dive.

Recovery from a spin can use up quite an amount of height, which makes it a very unhealthy situation to be in low down. Modern light aeroplanes and particularly microlights are not prone to fully developed spins; they simply start one – known as an incipient spin – and then pack in the whole idea! Any aeroplane, however, will spin if sufficiently provoked and recovery will require that the rotation is arrested prior to recovering from the stall; prevention is better than cure!

Most of these aeroplanes have a facility called wash-out to reduce the chance of a spin. Wash-out is a decrease in the 'angle of incidence' (a built-in angle of attack on the wing in relation to the datum line of the aeroplane) at the tips compared with that at the roots. Thus, as a high angle of attack begins to bring on a stall, the inboard parts of the wing stall first leaving the tips still 'flying'.

However, the fact that a spin may be relatively difficult to induce in no way excuses you from maintaining the utmost vigilance over airspeed close to the stall – you could just end up proving your aeroplane is able to spin after all and find yourself 'up to your wings in aerodrome!'

Loading

Previously we have seen that centripetal force (CF) provides the required horizontal force for a turn.

Now every force must produce an equal and opposite reaction otherwise the object being acted upon would be constantly on the move and never achieve a balanced state.

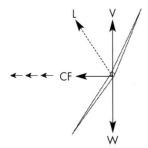

Figure 3.84

In Figure 3.84 you can see how W is the force that stops V continuing to take the aeroplane upwards.

So, in a balanced turn there is a force acting outwards to balance centripetal force and this is called **Centrifugal Reaction** (CR) – known by some perhaps wrongly as centrifugal force. Anyway, we will talk about it as a force where it suits. (Figure 3.85).

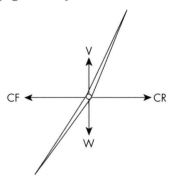

Figure 3.85

The best way to understand this force is to imagine how a stone whirled around your head on a string is constantly trying to fly off but is held by the string. Centrifugal reaction is the force that keeps the string taut as long as the whirling continues with adequate speed.

Next imagine you are seated in a 'Chair-o-plane' at the fairground. Whilst at rest your weight acts vertically down through the seat. As the chair is set in motion it moves outwards from rest and continues to do so as long as speed is increasing.

Now think about your body as all this is going on. You are pressed further and further into the seat until you cannot move even if you want to; it is as if your weight has increased enormously. In fact you are being subjected to the combination of your own weight and centrifugal reaction (Figure 3.86 on page 47).

The combination or resultant of the two forces CR and W is the diagonal of the parallelogram they can form. The force (or reaction) represented by the diagonal acts straight through the seat at whatever angle you find yourself and it is known as **Loading** (LG). (Figure 3.87 on page 47).

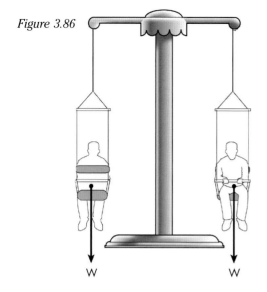

Figure 3.86

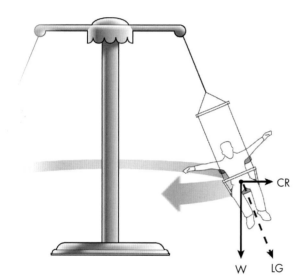

In fact at 60° of bank the loading is equivalent to ×2, which means you feel twice as heavy as you really are. This experience of feeling heavier is as if the force of gravity ('g') has increased. When stationary we feel the normal effects of gravity (1 'g') and when we are at 60° of bank we experience twice the force of gravity (2 'g').

From Figure 3.87 we can now arrive at a conclusion. Since CR = CF and W = V, then it is obvious that LG must = L.

Hence, when lift is increased to make a balanced turn the loading will go up at the same rate. Referring back to Figure 3.82 and taking the lift increases at the different angles depicted therein, another table can be produced which translates into the 'weight' of the pilot for the same situations. On this occasion L is replaced by LG.

Table 3.3

Angle of bank	Loading factor	Pilot weight		Actual loading
0°	1.0	x	168 lb (76Kg) =	168 lb (76Kg)
15°	1.04	x	168 lb (76Kg) =	175 lb (79Kg)
30°	1.16	x	168 lb (76Kg) =	195 lb (88Kg)
60°	2.0	x	168 lb (76Kg) =	336 lb (152Kg)

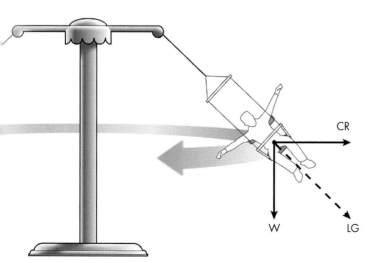

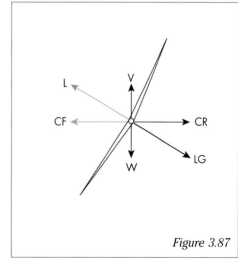

Figure 3.87

Manoeuvring and Loading

A few final points to learn about the turn as a manoeuvre and about loading are as follows:

– To produce the lift required to maintain a steep turn could require increased airspeed that is well beyond the aeroplane's power to produce. The outcome can be a stall and spin if you attempt it – due to increased induced drag.

– It is not only the pilot 'weight' that increases with loading. The whole aeroplane undergoes the stress. Increase the loading beyond the aeroplane's design limit and it can break up in mid-air.

– Loading is not only increased in a turn but also in such manoeuvres as a loop, where it can be particularly high when pulling out at the bottom.

Manoeuvring Speed

So far we have looked at loading in the sense of being careful not to induce manoeuvres which over-stress the aeroplane.

Unfortunately nature can create situations whereby loads can be induced over which you have no control.

The weather can be very fickle and unforgiving in the form of turbulence, where violent gusts can exist which strike with alarming rapidity and with the force of a sledge-hammer.

When the sea is really rough the sailor hauls in the sails to minimise the area exposed to the wind. This move also slows down the boat so that it meets any adverse force with the minimum impact.

An aeroplane cannot haul in any sails but it can reduce its speed to achieve the same end.

The maximum airspeed at which a given aeroplane is adjudged to be capable of accepting full control inputs and handling rough air is known as its **Manoeuvring Speed** – it should be rigidly adhered to where conditions warrant it.

Summary

In drawing to a close on this subject of principles of flight there are a few points worthy of emphasis.

– Without sufficient airspeed you cannot fly – you will stall.

– Increased airspeed is vital in banked manoeuvres. The steeper the bank, the greater the stalling speed.

– A stall near the ground may not leave you with sufficient height in which to regain flying speed.

– A stall off the turn will leave you with even less height in which to recover.

Watch your airspeed and you will be able to enjoy watching it over many happy years of flying.

Chapter 4
Power and Ancillaries

Types of Power Plant

A hesitant old dear at an air show once asked. 'Young man, why does your machine have that big fan in the front?' 'Madam', replied the intrepid flyer – 'it's to keep me cool up there.'

'You're pulling my leg, sir' – was the sharp retort. 'Maybe', said the pilot thoughtfully – 'But you should see how hot I get when it stops!'

An old chestnut perhaps, but it sums up a lot. An in-depth knowledge of engines is not necessary to become a good pilot. What does matter is knowing what can make them stop so that you are able to take precautions against it ever happening and that is the main purpose of this section.

Few people taking up flying are unaware of the basics in engine operation – that is, the **Four-Stroke Cycle** (Figures 4.1–4).

Induction
- Inlet valve opens

- Fuel mixture is sucked in as piston goes down the cylinder

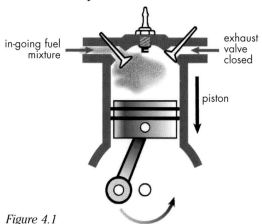

Figure 4.1

Compression
- Inlet valve closes

- Fuel mixture is compressed at top of cylinder as piston returns up the cylinder

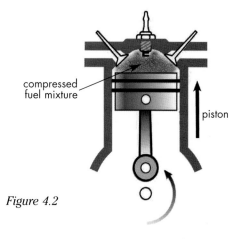

Figure 4.2

Power
- Mixture is ignited by spark-plug at the end of the compression stroke

- Expanding hot gases drive piston back down cylinder imparting power to a driveshaft

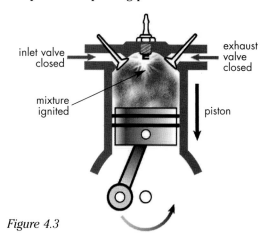

Figure 4.3

49

Exhaust

- Outlet valve opens

- Burnt gases escape – assisted by piston returning up the cylinder

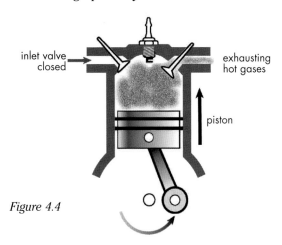

Figure 4.4

The **Two-Stroke Cycle**, very relevant to micro-lights, does the same thing but much faster (Figures 4.5–6).

Compression/Induction

- Fuel mixture already induced into top of cylinder is compressed as piston goes up

- Simultaneously a new supply of fuel mixture is induced through inlet into crankcase

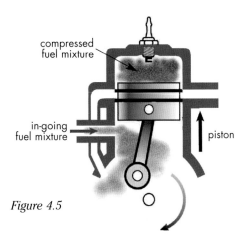

Figure 4.5

Power/Exhaust

- Mixture is ignited by spark-plug at the end of the compression stroke

- Expanding hot gases drive piston back down cylinder imparting power to drive shaft

- Simultaneously the exhaust outlet is exposed allowing burnt gases to escape

- At the same time the bypass inlet is also exposed and the down-going piston expels new fuel mixture from the crankcase through bypass to top of cylinder.

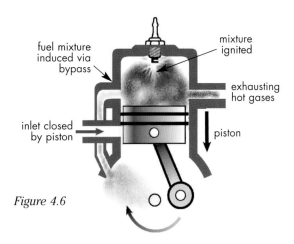

Figure 4.6

Cylinder Arrangement

Engines with more than one cylinder are described according to their cylinder layout as follows (Figure 4.7).

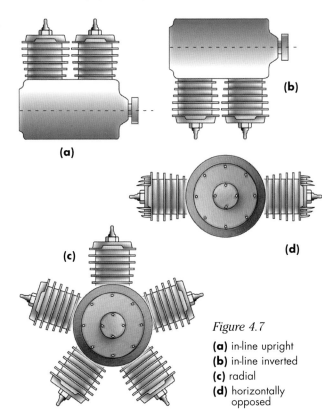

Figure 4.7

(a) in-line upright
(b) in-line inverted
(c) radial
(d) horizontally opposed

In each of the above cases you can see that the cylinders have fins around them which dissipate heat into the airflow.

Sometimes a fan is used to blow air over the hot cylinders as well as relying on the airflow.

Either way, such engines are known as **Air Cooled**.

Cylinders can be enclosed in a sealed jacket or casing containing water or other specified liquids. The heat is dissipated through a radiator as in a car and the engine in this case is described as **Liquid Cooled**.

Cylinders which become too hot can lead to an engine seizure. It is therefore essential not to modify your motor in a manner that in any way shields a cylinder from the airflow.

Useful additions can be instruments such as a **cylinder head temperature (CHT) gauge**, whose function is self evident by its name, or an **exhaust gas temperature (EGT) gauge**. Both will give warning of impending problems.

Lubrication

A four-stroke engine is lubricated by a separate oil system where oil is pumped to all the vital moving parts.

Never assume you have enough oil. Always carry out a physical check. Just enough is not enough; never take off without the oil tank being fully topped up.

The two-stroke engine lubricates itself as it runs. Oil is mixed with the fuel – petrol in this case – in carefully measured proportions such as 50 parts fuel to 1 part of oil. The ratio here is said to be 50:1.

From lubrication by pre-mixed fuel (petrol/oil) the two-stroke is turning to direct oil injection. If you happen to have this system, ensure that the oil tank is always full – but **not** with pre-mixed fuel.

Pay particular attention to the engine manufacturer's handbook as to the ratio required. Mistakes in this area can be costly.

It goes without saying that the correct grade of oil should always be used. Care should be taken to avoid mixing different based oils.

Fuel

Light aeroplanes with their four-stroke engines normally use aviation fuel – AVGAS as it is called. This fuel is available at all main aerodromes and some private landing strips. AVGAS is available in a variety of grades, the most frequently available options are 100LL (low lead) or 91UL (unleaded). The filler source for AVGAS 100LL will be coloured **red** and contains a **blue** dye.

As a matter of interest Jet Fuel source points are coloured **black**.

AVGAS is much more expensive than ordinary car petrol and obtaining it also calls for visiting an aerodrome with all the attendant charges this implies.

Microlights can use unleaded fuel to BS (EN) 228: 1995 standard – you can call it unleaded MOGAS. Practically all microlights can run on it; if you are at all unhappy, check your aeroplane manual. This fuel must **not** be stored for any length of time as it likes to absorb water. Unlike microlight engines, most conventional aero engines cannot use unleaded MOGAS.

Fuel Problems

With the emphasis being on 'trouble-shooting' we will now look at the problems that can arise in a fuel system.

Amount of Fuel

Running out of fuel does happen. Just as you must do with oil, physically check your fuel prior to take-off – do not rely on gauges alone.

Dirt in Fuel

The easiest way to undergo spontaneous 'engine-off' landing practice is to allow only the smallest particle of grit to find its way into your carburettor fuel jet.

When filling up from cans instead of the pump at an aerodrome refuelling point, you run the risk of dirt entering the system.

Ensure you are equipped with the very best filter you can lay your hands on.

Water Contamination

Water can unintentionally find its way into a fuel system apart from heavy rain taking place during filling.

Should a fuel tank be left empty or partially so for any length of time, the moisture in the air within the tank can condense and the water so formed will settle at the bottom of the tank – water being heavier than petrol.

Some tanks are fitted with a drain cock at the bottom. As part of a preflight check, the pilot releases a sample of fuel into a glass container. Any water present will immediately identify itself at the bottom of the glass. If water is present, fuel should be drained off until no water is present in the sample.

Because water is heavier than petrol, should there be any other part of the fuel system at a lower point than the tank, then any water found in the tank could also be in that lower part of the system, so take no chances.

The risk of condensation can be reduced by keeping tanks full and/or not leaving the aeroplane outdoors all night where the colder night air can cause condensation.

Venting

Fuel can only flow through the system if it can be replaced by air as it leaves the tank.

A completely sealed tank will not permit free movement of fuel as, if it could do so, a vacuum (no air area) would be set up and atmospheric pressure outside the tank would at once push the fuel back inside.

To avoid this situation, all tanks are provided with a vent in the filler cap or directly into the tank itself. Always check that vents are free from obstruction as any blockage could restrict fuel flow into the carburettor.

Carburation

The carburettor is responsible for supplying the correct mixture of fuel and air into the combustion chamber of the cylinder in amounts varying according to the power desired.

Fuel is gravity-fed or pumped into a float

chamber which, by means of a needle valve closing the fuel inlet, always contains just the right amount of fuel required at a given time (Figure 4.8).

fuel flows into float chamber

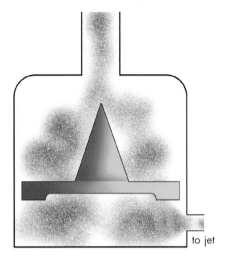

to jet

float rises with intake of fuel and needle blocks entry of fuel

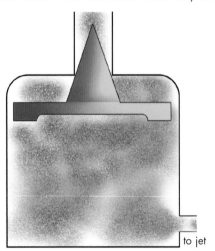

to jet

Figure 4.8

Fuel must now be mixed with air to provide the correct mixture. This takes place when air sucked in by piston movement also sucks neat fuel out of the float chamber.

The suction effect is increased because the air passes through a venturi and a reduction in pressure takes place as it speeds up through this restriction (refer back to Chapter 3 Principles of Flight for explanation of venturi effect).

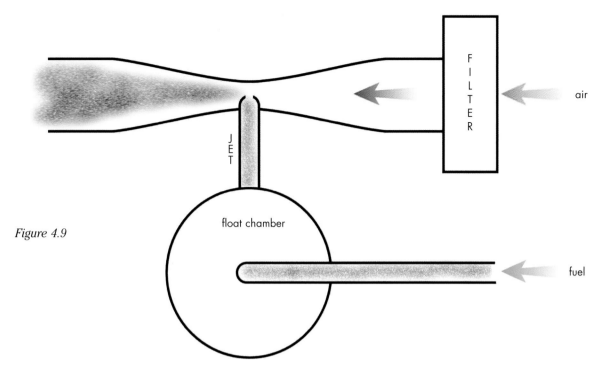

Figure 4.9

As the fuel passes from the float chamber to the venturi it flows through a fixed jet. Jets can be of various sizes according to the requirements of a particular engine.

The larger the bore of the jet, the richer the mixture will be. Picture the smallest particle of dirt clogging a jet and you can see why the emphasis is on filtering fuel. Filtering the air intake is also a good move as dirt in a cylinder shortens engine life.

The above operation is depicted in Figure 4.9.

The fuel very quickly vaporises on its way to the combustion chamber to form the highly inflammable mixture needed.

The amount of power is controlled by the amount of mixture admitted into the combustion chamber. This function can be performed in two ways.

On four-stroke engines it is usually in the form of a butterfly valve placed in the path of the mixture on its route from the carburettor to the cylinder. Butterflies can also be found with two-stroke engines (Figure 4.10).

On many two-strokes the mixture amount admitted is controlled by a plunger which moves up and down in the air intake opening or closing the intake accordingly. Attached to the plunger is a needle valve which regulates the amount of neat fuel admitted to match the amount of air being let through (Figure 4.11).

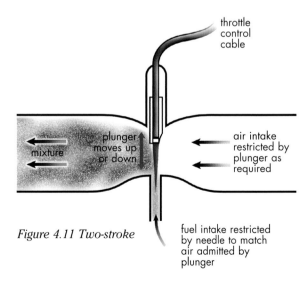

Figure 4.11 Two-stroke

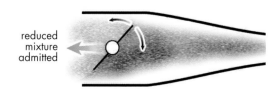

Figure 4.10 Four-stroke

Mixture Problems

Apart from an obstructed jet there are other factors which can influence the efficiency of the fuel mixture introduced into the combustion chamber.

Air Density

If the density of the air should decrease then it means that less air will be flowing through the venturi to mix with the fuel.

This results in a relatively higher proportion of fuel to air or in aviation parlance – a richer mixture.

The outcome of this situation can be a reduction in power – not a nice thought on take-off from a short field.

Air becomes less dense as altitude increases or as temperature increases.

Translating this into practical terms it means – watch out when using high altitude airfields and/or taking off in high temperatures.

Humidity

Although not to the same degree as altitude and temperature the humidity of the air can affect density. If the air has a very high water vapour content, it will in fact be less dense than drier air.

Mixture Control

In flight the problem will progress with every foot of altitude you gain as you climb into less dense air.

To a certain extent any loss of power through rich running can be combated by fitting mixture control.

This control reduces the amount of fuel introduced into the venturi so that correct proportions are maintained between fuel and air.

This process is known as 'leaning off' the mixture. However, be careful in creating too lean a mixture. Fuel has a cooling effect and if it is not present in sufficient amounts the engine will begin to 'run hot' and the possibility of a piston seizure is introduced.

The process of leaning off as you climb has its limits. In reducing the amount of fuel to match the reduced amount of air due to less density,

you are ending up with an overall less dense mixture which in turn produces less power. Whilst the fitting of a supercharger to ram additional air into the system will delay the effect, you will find that every engine reaches the stage where it is no longer producing enough power to sustain flight. However, we are now talking of altitudes way outside the normal environment of microlights or light aircraft.

Carburettor Icing

In talking about fuel mixture we seem to have made some incursions into the realms of meteorology with all the references to air density and humidity.

Discussing carb-icing as it is familiarly known must also be along the same lines.

Cause

When pressure decreases, so does temperature. Also, when evaporation takes place, temperature drops.

In a carburettor the decrease in pressure brought about by the venturi, coupled with the evaporation of fuel as it enters the airflow, both combine to bring about a sharp drop in temperature which can be as much as 33° C in a fraction of a second.

If the drop should take the temperature in the carburettor to below 0°C, which is freezing point, then any water particles produced by condensation due to cooling can at once turn to ice.

The ice can build up in sufficient amounts to restrict the intake of mixture into the cylinder to the extent that not only is power lost but there could be a complete engine failure (Figure 4.12).

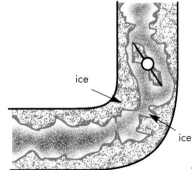

Figure 4.12

Conditions Favourable for Carb-Icing

If the outside air temperature is well below freezing point any condensation will turn into ice crystals which will not adhere to the interior of the intake but be ingested into the combustion chamber thus presenting no problem.

There will be no problem either on days when the air is very dry when there is insufficient water vapour to be condensed.

However, conditions conducive to carb-icing are far from infrequent. It can occur any time the air is moist enough and the outside temperature is between –7° and 21°C.

Risk is at a peak during low or closed throttle settings. Reducing this risk will be discussed shortly.

Indications of Carb-Icing

The first indication, if you have a fixed pitched propeller, will be a drop in rpm (engine revolutions per minute) as the mixture intake is restricted.

Later will come a roughness in engine running.

Carb Heating

The purpose of carb heating is to prevent ice building up in the carburettor and finally blocking the fuel flow to the piston chamber. Whatever type is used on a microlight, the general idea is to warm the carb casing and so melt any ice beginning to form.

It is worth mentioning that most light aircraft use a very different form of carb heater which directs air from the engine into the venturi. While this will de-ice a carburettor very quickly, it also causes significant power loss; as a result it is normally only used at low power and during flight in known icing conditions. This system is not normally found on microlight aeroplanes.

Problems with Carb Heating

Cures are not without cost. Introduce warm air which is less dense and you end up with a mixture which is less dense. This means a loss in power and a further drop in rpm.

As the ice clears there will be a rise in rpm

which will often be accompanied by intermittent rough running as the engine swallows the ice.

When the control is taken off and all ice is gone, the rpm will rise to a higher setting than before its application and the engine will run smoothly.

Because low or closed throttle settings increase the risk of carb-icing, do watch out when descending from height with an idling engine. If you suspect conditions are ripe for carb-icing make sure you open up the throttle periodically for a few seconds. This will ensure you are keeping some heat available to use from an engine which would otherwise be cooling fast.

Finally, make sure that carb heat control is not applied on take-off and landing when the availability of full power is critical. However, if a maker's handbook tells you otherwise then naturally you must abide by its instructions.

Fuel Injection

Fuel may also be supplied directly into the cylinders of the engine by a fuel pump in conjunction with a control unit. Fuel injection avoids many of the issues associated with conventional carburettors as well the prospect of improved fuel efficiency.

Ignition

Having carefully nursed the correct mixture all the way to the combustion chamber, it is now time to blow it up!

In actual fact the process is one of progressive burning but at very high speed.

Ignition is the job of a spark-plug which fires just prior to the piston reaching the top of the cylinder so that the maximum impact from detonation of the mixture takes effect as the piston commences its downward stroke.

Figure 4.13

The spark is generated by an electrical discharge jumping from one electrode to another. The gap between the electrodes is critical so always ensure it is that laid down by the manufacturers.

Too small a gap and the spark may be insufficient to ignite the mixture. Too large and the discharge may not have the strength to jump it – hence no spark (Figure 4.13).

Temperature and mixture play an important part in the efficient operation of a plug.

Too low a temperature and/or a rich fuel mixture can cause a carbon deposit to build up between the electrodes.

Too high a temperature can damage the electrodes apart from other damage to piston and cylinder.

In a two-stroke engine an added problem can be the oil content in the mixture. If burning is inefficient the electrodes can become wet coated in oil and this insulates them thus preventing a spark – making starting difficult.

This problem is magnified if the cylinder is of the inverted format. The unburnt oil falls into the plug and floods it.

Should you be running in a new engine at an initially higher oil to fuel ratio – say 30:1 instead of 50:1 – then with an inverted engine you may find it best to remove the plug after flight and allow residual oil to drip out. If you do not follow this course of action you may find it impossible to start the engine.

Finally, damp can play havoc with plug leads. Often this problem can be overcome by spraying with a proprietary liquid spray, but check that they are worth spraying. Replacement may be what is really needed.

Dual Ignition

Four-stroke engines used in aeroplanes normally have two spark-plugs per cylinder – each being fired by a separate magneto.

Having two sparks in each cylinder ensures maximum burning of the mixture and therefore maximum power for a given throttle setting.

Also, having two of everything means there is a back-up system if one of the two should go wrong.

Prior to take-off each magneto is tested on its own as well as both together.

There will be an acceptable drop in rpm when the engine is running on one magneto as only one out of the two plugs in each cylinder will be firing and therefore power output will not be so great.

Should this drop exceed the acceptable drop laid down for the particular type of engine then you have a problem – either with a plug or the magneto itself.

Some two-stroke engines have two plugs per cylinder but they are both fired from a common source. The benefit of a twin spark is enjoyed and also the back-up facility should one fail. However, if anything goes wrong with the magneto then your prowess as a glider pilot comes to the fore.

Master Switch

The definition 'master switch' may give the impression that it controls everything – that nothing will work when it is 'off'. This is not true; it controls the battery and therefore all that depends on this power source and in some cases the alternator or generator.

It does not affect the engine or its primary system – a propeller swing can still start an engine even if the master switch is 'off'.

Ignition Switch

The ignition switch controls the firing – or not – of the engine and it does so in what may seem to be an odd sort of way. It does so by being totally ineffective when in the 'on' position thus allowing firing of plugs to occur.

When switched 'off' it starts to perform its function of earthing the coil or primary windings of the magneto so that the engine cannot fire.

Fire Hazard

When fuel mixture and ignition get together there is always a risk of fire.

In the event of fire, the fuel system should be turned 'off' at once along with the ignition switch.

However, should the fire be in the engine you should delay switching off the ignition. By doing so the engine will continue to operate and use up the fuel remaining in proximity to the fire.

When the residual fuel is used up the ignition switch should be turned to 'off' and hopefully the fire will die down as there is no fuel to burn.

Exhaust System

The exhaust system is the means whereby the burnt gases in the combustion chamber are expelled into the air from the engine.

Vital to the system is the silencer as without it the noise would be unbearable.

With a two-stroke engine the noise potential can be very considerable. Not only does it run at a much higher rpm than a four-stroke but emission of exhaust is at twice the rate due to its operating cycle.

Silencers are carefully designed to match the engine so modifications are out unless approved by the makers.

Unburnt oil in a two-stroke mixture can clog up holes in a silencer and restrict the exhaust gas flow. This can cause back pressure leading to a reduction in power.

Again, always ensure you use the right mixture so as to minimise this possibility.

The Propeller

A propeller is no more than a revolving aerofoil generating lift which pulls or pushes the aeroplane through the air.

The principle is depicted below in Figure 4.14.

Notice how the angle of the propeller blade progressively lessens from the root to the tip.

Lift increases with both airspeed and angle of attack. To ensure the 'lift' force produced is uniform from root to tip for a given propeller revolution, the angle of the blade is:

– Higher at the root where blade speed is lowest

– Lower at the tip where blade speed is highest.

Propeller Arrangement

There are two propeller arrangements to consider – tractor and pusher.

The first pulls the aeroplane through the air; the other pushes as the name implies.

Tractor

The tractor format has certain points worth noting. The airflow from the propeller – slipstream as it is called – increases the airspeed over the inboard surfaces of the wings. This produces extra lift in that area, but be careful that the outboard surfaces do not stall whilst you are making use of the 'inboard bonus' at low airspeed (Figure 4.15).

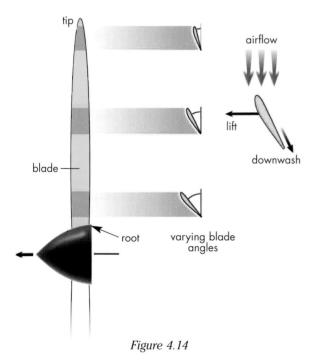

Figure 4.14

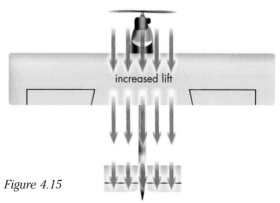

Figure 4.15

Snags with this form of layout are the increased airflow around the pilot's face in an open cockpit – unless there is a well-designed windscreen – and visibility can be impaired somewhat.

Pusher

The tractor snags disappear in this format but so does the increased lift.

The effect is most marked in the sensitivity of control by the tail unit surfaces of rudder and elevator – but, only as long as power is applied (Figure 4.16).

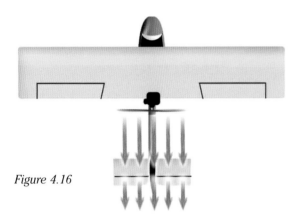

Figure 4.16

Propeller Care

Maximum efficiency demands a smooth-running perfectly balanced propeller.

The slightest imbalance will at once introduce vibration and along with this comes the loosening of nuts, screws and so forth but more importantly – fatigue.

There is every chance that the cause of imbalance will be damage to a blade.

Taxiing over rough ground will see small stones quickly sent up into the propeller arc. Even mud or soft earth will damage high revving blades.

Propellers are often protected to a certain extent by metal or plastic sheeting around the leading edge of the blades.

Apart from imbalance caused by nicks or wear on blades it must be remembered that the propeller at high speed is very brittle and will easily crack – if not totally break up – on contact with the smallest of objects.

Examine your propeller regularly and thoroughly and any signs of undue wear or cracks must be treated as highly suspect.

Propellers made up of laminated layers of wood must be examined for the possibility of de-lamination taking place where layers are joined.

Propeller Failure

You will be left in no doubt if your propeller fails – the engine will run away to highly unacceptable revs. Damage can be caused to the engine if power is not shut down quickly enough together with selecting 'Ignition Off' the instant it happens. Vibration will be very great.

Before adopting a high speed glide, a cursory glance round and check on controls should be carried out in case damage has been caused to the structure of the aeroplane. If you even suspect such damage, keep airspeed down to a minimum to ease loading on the machine as it descends for a forced landing.

Fitting

Contrary to some beliefs, fitting a propeller the wrong way round will not see you disappearing into reverse on starting up.

What you will experience is a decline in thrust as the effect of camber on the blade in producing lift will be lost (Figure 4.17).

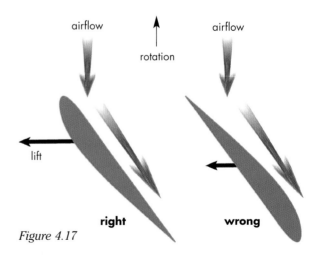

airflow

rotation

airflow

lift

right

wrong

Figure 4.17

Reduction Gear

We have touched on the fact that the propeller tip travels very much faster than the root.

In fact, a 36-in diameter propeller rotating at 6500 rpm is bordering on supersonic speed at the tip, which is travelling at some 735 mph. That tip only has to go supersonic (760 mph at sea level) to create the most unacceptable noise as it goes through the 'sound barrier'.

Also, as mentioned before, a propeller at high speed is in its most brittle state and susceptible to damage from the least thing in its path – apart from any existing defects which may have weakened it.

Both problems can be eased by slowing the speed of the propeller but in such a way that there is no loss in thrust.

This is achieved by means of reduction gear, where the direct drive engine revolutions are reduced to less than half at the point of propeller drive.

The thrust can be maintained – and sometimes increased – by using a larger propeller.

The format of reduction drive as opposed to direct drive is shown in Figure 4.18.

The days of 'belt'-driven reduction have virtually given way to the gearbox system which forms an integral part of the engine. On a pre-flight check with the engine off, watch out for excessive propeller 'freeplay' and/or noise – signs that the cog teeth within the box are becoming worn.

Should you happen to be still operating on the belt system, then check the belt regularly for both tension and condition; also ensure it is not slipping and causing a loss in engine power.

It is possible to change the gear ratio of either type of reduction system by changing either pulleys or gearsets; but take care that a change does not invalidate your permit to fly!

The actual power delivered by the combination of the engine, propeller and, if applicable, reduction drive will be less than the nominal power output of the engine, as the thrust delivery system is not completely efficient. Whilst the power output of the engine may be quoted in brake horsepower, the power output from the propeller will be defined in terms of thrust horsepower.

Tyre Care/Wheels/Heavy Landings

Tyres tend to become overlooked as they are not vital to flight; however, on take-off and landing they are critical.

Superficial nicks and cuts or scoring may not seem too much of a problem but among them may be a deep one which renders that tyre unfit for use.

Certainly any tyre with the casing exposed must be changed at once. However, baldness in a tyre designed specifically for aircraft is

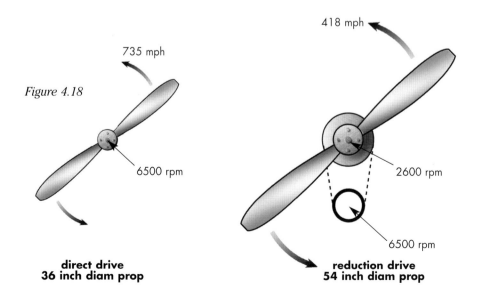

Figure 4.18

735 mph

6500 rpm

**direct drive
36 inch diam prop**

418 mph

2600 rpm

6500 rpm

**reduction drive
54 inch diam prop**

acceptable to a certain degree but not for any length of time. Maintaining correct pressure goes without saying.

Whilst on the subject of wheels, it is worth mentioning the effect a grass surface can have – particularly where the diameter is small.

As grass grows it will have a progressive effect on your take-off run by lengthening it – more so if it is wet. Given the small fields that a microlight can use, makes watching this point essential. If your propeller begins to look as if it has been dipped in green dye you can assume the grass is too long and you are operating a lawn mower rather than an aeroplane.

Mud or newly mown hay can play havoc if you have fitted spats – they clog up easily and can be worse than brakes being applied at the wrong moment.

Finally, still on the subject of wheels, a word on heavy landings. Such occurrences happen to everyone and human nature makes many pilots relieved that no one saw them!

Such an attitude could not be more dangerous. A quick cursory glance at the wheels, the straightening of the odd tube and going into the air once more could mean serious problems.

The shock of a heavy landing may break an undercarriage – in a way this is a good thing. It will mean the wheels could well have absorbed the entire shock.

On the other hand, if they are reasonably intact you must ask yourself – where did the shock go? It has almost certainly been transmitted up through the remainder of the airframe.

So, never hide your heavy landings. Assume that damage has been done and ensure an inspection is carried out on all areas which could be affected before you fly again. Incidentally, it is a legal requirement that you enter such incidents in your aircraft log book where they can be noted on inspection.

Sailcloth

With the advent of the Dacron/aluminium technology which is so prevalent in microlight aeroplanes it was initially boasted that the Dacron had an indefinite life.

In fact, the average sailcloth used can have a very long life as long as it is not left exposed to sunlight over any length of time.

The ultra-violet content of daylight causes gradual deterioration to cloth and stitching. An immediate and obvious sign is fading of colour.

A deliberate test for any weakening is to press your thumb down on the surface and if an indentation remains then you could have a problem. Again, drawing the back of your thumbnail along the stitching will tell a tale. If it breaks down into a powder it is finished.

Although the sail must always be inspected at the annual permit renewal, if you are unsure about the safety of the sail at any time then immediately set about a sail check with an inspector, the manufacturer of the aeroplane or a microlight sailmaker.

After all, it is the only means by which you are able to descend from a height at your own discretion. If the cloth should fail, your rate of descent will be that of a discontented breeze-block!

With regard to the powered parachute, the canopy can react adversely to sunlight in the same way as the sailcloth can degrade on a normal microlight aeroplane; it should be stowed away in a bag when not in use. A wet canopy should be thoroughly dried before being stowed away.

The suspension and control lines on a canopy can be susceptible to chafing so they should be frequently inspected for damage; also all connector links should be checked often and tightened prior to flight if found to be loose.

Corrosion

Corrosion is another means by which an aeroplane can deteriorate. An eye should be kept on corrosion – particularly around nuts and bolts together with flying and control cables.

Time may account for corrosion in many cases but it can be considerably accelerated in others by exterior factors such as spillage of acid from a battery. Such acid coming into contact with the aeroplane or rubber tyres should be washed down swiftly in some neutralising solution such as sodium bicarbonate.

On no account must metal parts in an aeroplane be protected with any kind of paint or surface treatment; many such paints are specifically designed to hide cracks or corrosion. While this is a good idea on the wing of a car it is extremely stupid to do so on a vital part of an aeroplane.

Metal Fatigue

The most common cause of damage to metal aircraft parts is metal fatigue. This happens when a small crack occurs – perhaps at a bolt hole, a bend or often inside a weld. It can be virtually unnoticed at the outset but in time it will grow sufficiently to cause a part to break – for example, lines of oil or grease appearing in surface dust. Fatigue most often occurs on parts which undergo constant flexing such as undercarriages and engine mounts.

If you suspect any fatigue crack during an inspection, maintenance or at any time – in fact if you see any crack at all – on no account fly the aeroplane until it has been investigated. It may be possible to stop a crack expanding by drilling a small hole at its tip. This can be acceptable in a sheet-metal panel, but with any other part such as tubing or brackets, forget the drill and change the part.

Conclusion

It was said at the beginning of this chapter that your knowledge needs to be such that you prevent problems rather than be an expert in putting them right after they have occurred.

Digest what you have just read and you will fly more confidently and safely.

Chapter 5
Basic Flight Instruments

We now look at the use and working principles of four basic flight instruments – the altimeter, airspeed indicator, vertical speed indicator and magnetic compass. The diagrams will not necessarily represent the actual mechanism inside each one but they will give you an idea of the principles involved in their working.

The Altimeter
This crucial instrument is closely related to atmospheric pressure, and therefore its uses, as opposed to its method of operation, are dealt with later in Chapter 8 Meteorology.

Figure 5.1 Clockwise from top left: Vertical Speed Indicator (VSI); Airspeed Indicator (ASI); Altimeter; Rev. Counter; Engine Hours Meter; Cylinder Head Temperature Gauge

The altimeter is the instrument which indicates the height of the aircraft above a pre-selected surface level.

It is nothing more than a sensitive aneroid barometer; but in this case it is calibrated to read feet instead of hectoPascals (hPa) or millibars (mb) on the basis that 1 hPa or mb change in pressure equates to a change of approximately 30 ft in terms of height. At the base is a knob which enables a selected pressure setting to be entered on the altimeter at any given time on the ground or in flight.

As opposed to meteorology, in this case atmospheric pressure is known as **static pressure**; it is fed to the instrument from an aperture set into the fuselage side so that it is at right angles to any airflow. (Figure 5.2).

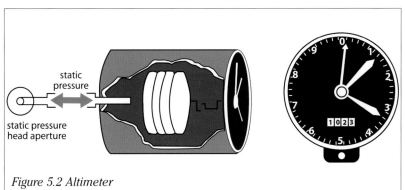

Figure 5.2 Altimeter

As you can see, the altimeter can have a three-handed dial. The first and largest will indicate height in 00s of feet; the second smaller one will show height in 000s of feet, and the third and smallest with a ring on it depicts height 0,000s of feet. This format has led to mis-reading on a number of occasions so be particularly careful in your interpretations. It must be said in passing that whilst the occasional record breaker may need it, the idea of the average microlight pilot requiring a reading from the third and smallest hand certainly stretches the imagination!

Airspeed Indicator (ASI)

The ASI, as it is usually called, does just what its name implies – tells you your speed through the air but not over the ground as you will see in Chapter 9 Navigation.

Quite simply, oncoming air in flight enters a forward-facing aperture on the aircraft known as the pitot tube. It is carried through a line to a capsule in the instrument which can expand or contract. The pressure this air exerts on the capsule is a combination of static pressure (already there) and the additional pressure attributed to the

moving air, known as **dynamic pressure**. The effect of the1se two pressures is called the **total pressure**.

There is a need to ensure that the capsule, and thereby the reading, is only influenced by *dynamic* pressure – the moving air. To this end, a static pressure line is also introduced into this instrument which exerts itself on the *outside* of the capsule.

This nullifies the static pressure content of the total pressure *inside* the capsule. The net effect is that in the end only the required dynamic pressure is linked from the capsule to the dial where it is registered in terms of **statute miles** per hour **(mph)** or **nautical miles** per hour which are **knots (kt)** (Figure 5.3).

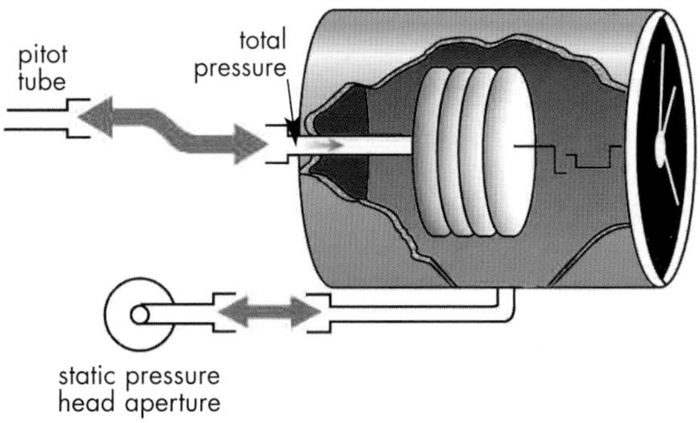

Figure 5.3 Airspeed Indicator (ASI)

A reading on an ASI is known as the **Indicated Airspeed** and can be subject to a number of effects: positioning, altitude and temperature.

Positioning
Should the pitot head be out of line with the airflow, or subject to disruption by part of the aircraft structure, the dynamic pressure will be distorted.

Similar distortion can occur when the line from the pitot head is 'kinked' by a fastener or too sharp a bend on its route to the ASI.

Altitude

At high altitude the density of the atmosphere is far less than at sea level. This will result in an overall reduction of both dynamic and static pressure.

But although the dynamic pressure in the capsule may now be less, its expansion will not decrease because the static pressure opposing it will also be less. The indicated airspeed thus remains constant.

However, the aircraft, in passing through less dense air, will be moving faster than the indicated speed for the same power owing to it meeting with less resistance.

Temperature

Temperature can have an effect on density at all levels and therefore have an effect on both dynamic and static pressure.

Pilots who need to fly on instruments alone, with no means of relating to the ground for visual position checks, can deal with the last two problems by use of a navigation computer which enables indicated airspeed to be converted into **True Airspeed**.

*There is a stage between indicated and true airspeed known as **Rectified Airspeed** where any correction for a particular instrument appears on a card in the cockpit.*

Vertical Speed Indicator (VSI)

The VSI indicates the rate at which an aircraft is climbing or descending in terms of feet per minute. Once again we have a capsule capable of expansion/contraction in the operation of this instrument; this time it is related to the speed at which pressure decreases or increases on climb or descent.

In this case static pressure has instant entry/exit to the capsule but its entry/exit to the area surrounding the capsule is only gradual due to the other aperture being restricted to deliberately delay movement either way (Figure 5.4).

In level flight the pressure both inside and outside the capsule will be the same, so the instrument will show a zero reading.

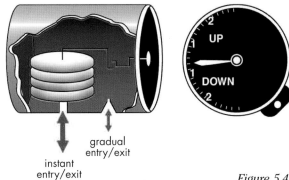

gradual entry/exit

instant entry/exit

*Figure 5.4
Vertical Speed Indicator (VSI)*

The operation in climb and descent is as follows:

Climb

Pressure in the capsule decreases as air *instantly* exits into the lower atmospheric pressure outside. Pressure on the capsule is now temporarily greater due to the pin-hole aperture allowing only a *gradual* exit of the air around it into the atmosphere.

The capsule therefore contracts under the greater pressure and the contraction is registered on the dial as rate of ascent.

Descent

Pressure in the capsule increases as air *instantly* enters the capsule from the higher atmospheric pressure outside.

Pressure on the capsule is temporarily less due to the pin-hole aperture allowing only a *gradual* entry of air into the capsule's surround.

The capsule therefore expands and the expansion is registered on the dial as rate of descent.

There is a minor problem with this instrument which calls for anticipation developed with practice. When the aircraft levels out after a climb or descent, the delay caused by the gradual entry/exit of air through the pin-hole aperture will continue to register a rate of climb/descent on the dial until pressure in the instrument has equalised with that in the capsule. At this time, when you have levelled out, pay attention to the altimeter otherwise you can end up 'chasing the VSI' in oscillating flight.

You may be wondering why, in the case of all the instruments covered, the static pressure line is fed to the exterior of the aircraft – why not just a hole in the instrument you might say?

The reason is simple. Should the instrument be housed in a heated cabin this will lead to a decrease in air density, in turn leading to a reduced pressure reading.

Altimeter, ASI and VSI Problems

The three instruments just discussed have one factor in common – they all rely on static pressure. With the relatively limited entry aperture on the static pressure line in terms of size it is very susceptible to blockage by the smallest particles of matter. Should this happen you could end up with false readings; static pressure inside the instrument will now be fixed and invariably differ from static pressure inside a capsule.

Icing can also be a problem when super-cooled liquid drops are ingested and freeze.

To enable these two problems to be overcome, many aircraft have an alternative interior static inlet. When necessary the line is switched to this internal aperture and allowance is then made for the effect of the reduced pressure mentioned earlier.

Perhaps it should be pointed out that such a nicety as an alternative static pressure inlet is unlikely to be found on many microlight aeroplanes – if any.

The ASI has an added problem with the dynamic pressure inlet in the form of the pitot tube having a much larger aperture. Not only can it pick up larger particles of matter in the air but it is also an excellent collector of rubbish on the ground thrown up by another aircraft running up in front of you or in close proximity.

This is overcome by the fitting of a sleeve cover over the pitot head at all times when the machine is not in use. But do make sure it is removed during your pre-flight check; fail to do so and you will have become one of many members of a club of pilots who have had the wind up them instead of through the pitot tube!

Again, because the pitot tube faces directly into the airflow it can ingest much more water in flight to encourage freezing – if icing conditions exist. The latter problem is solved on many aeroplanes by fitting a heated pitot head around the tube; but again, this is not likely to be found on microlights.

One final point; *never*, *ever*, blow into a pitot tube to check that an ASI is working – after doing so it probably won't!

The Magnetic Compass

The magnetic compass is well known to most people be they aviators or not. The magnetic field around the Earth converges on points close to the north and south geographic poles called the **Northern and Southern Magnetic Poles (NMP** and **SMP)**. Hence, a magnetised bar will always tend to point towards the NMP.

This principle enables the heading of an aircraft to be read off by a pilot against a fixed lubber line set against a needle or card linked to the magnetised bar. The readings will normally show N, S, E and W with the intervals between marked for each 30 degrees. Further sub-divisions between the 30 degree marks are shown for every 5 degrees. (Figure 5.5).

Figure 5.5 Magnetic Compass

To an aircraft in the air, the compass needle not only tends towards north but it will also tend downwards towards the NMP deep within the Earth until theoretically it would point vertically down when directly over it. This effect is known as magnet dip and, if fixed to its pivot point, the bar would jam up long before it reached such an extreme (Figure 5.6).

Figure 5.6 Magnet Dip

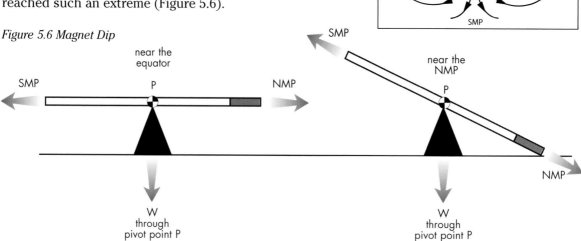

At the Equator the bar would remain horizontal, being under the influence of both NMP and SMP, but progress towards northern or southern latitudes will see the dip increase. To reduce this natural effect to a practical minimum, the bar is not fixed to its pivot point but is suspended from it. It now has the free movement of a pendulum in any direction.

point and acts against the dip effect. This counter-action is sufficient to limit dip to a mere few degrees of no consequence (Figure 5.7).

Figure 5.7 Dip Control

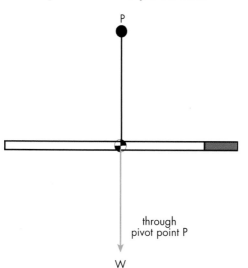

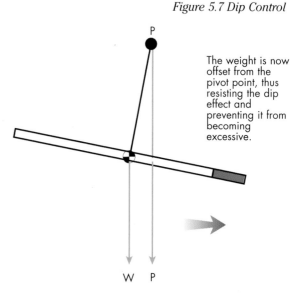

The weight is now offset from the pivot point, thus resisting the dip effect and preventing it from becoming excessive.

By adopting this method of suspension, as dip takes place the C of G of the bar is displaced; the weight now becomes offset from the pivot

So much for the workings of the magnetic compass.

Compass Problems

As with all instruments the magnetic compass has its own foibles of which you need to be aware, even if the reason escapes you or is never fully understood. There are times in flight when you can increase or decrease speed and notice a change in the indicated heading taking place without any sort of a turn having been initiated.

The same effect can be experienced in a turn when on rolling out a turn on to your new heading, the compass continues to move or else begins to reverse direction. In short, these effects can come about whenever you take your aircraft out of equilibrium (constant speed/height/heading).

With the former there is no need to do any-thing; the heading will revert back to normal when the aircraft settles down to its new speed – that is when equilibrium is restored. In the latter case remedial action can be taken to prevent you over- or under-correcting.

What causes all this to happen? The effects stem from the pendulum set-up, geared to pre-vent dip, which allows the C of G of the mag-netic bar to roam, for the want of a better word. This is just what it does as acceleration or deceleration takes place when an increase or decrease in speed is initiated.

Flying directly along a north/south line will show no change as the C of G movement will be along this axis. However, if flying from west to east or vice-versa then the offset C of G counteracting dip will hang back in accel-eration and move forward on deceleration. This causes the compass reading to deviate from the required heading until, as already said, equilibrium is restored (Figure 5.8).

When a turn is initiated another form of acceleration force (centripetal) is set up towards the centre of that turn. It is apart from any force introduced by a change in speed and this also adds to the problem of wander-ing headings due to the pendulum format of the bar. You can come out of a turn and find the compass reading under or over that

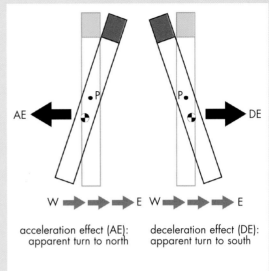

acceleration effect (AE): apparent turn to north

deceleration effect (DE): apparent turn to south

Figure 5.8 Acceleration/Deceleration Effect

required; in other words the needle is under or over shooting the lubber line. You should now appreciate that with changes in speed or direction there is an almost infinite number of permutations where the heading can stray from that required and the degree to which it may do so.

In a nutshell, where the turn is concerned it means that on rolling out of the turn when your compass reaches the required new heading, you must anticipate the afore-men-tioned effects. This is achieved by timing the manoeuvre just right to ensure the compass stops on the desired heading without repeated correction moves having to be made.

The degree to which these effects take place is governed by whether you are heading in an overall northerly or southerly direction when the turn is completed.

For a broad indication of what to do in a turn, remember:

– northerly: roll-out is made early
– southerly: roll-out is made late.

For an example, see the table 5.1 overleaf.

Finally, in the chapter which deals with Navigation and the **use** you make of compass readings, you will learn about the effect of deviation. This is caused through magnetic

Table 5.1

Initial Hdg.	New Hdg.	Roll-out at	
270	000	335	(early)
090	000	025	(early)
270	180	155	(late)
090	180	205	(late)

fields that are created by aircraft themselves. It is peculiar to each individual aircraft and the corrections in the calibrations should be visible in the cockpit on a deviation card. A new card is essential if any modifications are carried out, particularly when the changes or additions are made to electrical equipment.

Again, beware of any *additional* items of a metallic or electrical nature inadvertently placed near the compass during flight. Such items could be keyrings, transistor radios, mobile phones, metal map boards and so forth. They can contribute to errors in readings for which the deviation card has not allowed.

There are many more flight instruments we could discuss but they are mostly slanted towards blind flying in clouds or flight in keeping with IFR which is not part of the microlight scene.

Chapter 6
Air Law

Introduction

The sky may give the appearance of being empty. In reality it is very much occupied by considerable traffic moving at a variety of speeds ranging from nil to supersonic.

The body responsible for civil flight in the United Kingdom is the Civil Aviation Authority (CAA). The Authority is responsible to Parliament for the smooth, safe operation of such flight and it concerns itself not only with the safety of pilots, passengers and aeroplanes, but also with the safety of those on the ground over whom they fly.

Microlight flying is a relative newcomer to the aviation scene compared with other forms of flying. The simpler aeroplanes and minimal operational requirements therefore merited amendments to existing rules in order that the sport could function in a sensible manner.

The amendments have not only taken into consideration the safety aspects, but have made the attainment of a pilot's licence a less forbidding procedure. For example, the introduction of a 'restricted' licence caters for the would-be flyer who simply wishes to fly locally with no aspirations 'to boldly go where no man has gone before' – in other words, one who does not wish to go cross-country flying to any great extent.

As a consequence, there are many aspects of the Air Navigation Order (ANO) to which the microlight pilot and aeroplane owner must conform, but which may not appear in most other aviation text books on the subject.

European harmonisation of aviation procedures is the responsibility of the body known as the European Aviation Safety Agency (EASA), which makes recommendations to the institutions of the European Union (EU).

For some years after the beginning of European integration in aviation, microlights maintained their national individuality, but the definition has since been standardised across the EU. From 1st July 2002, the Microlight Licence became a 'Rating' in the National Private Pilots Licence (NPPL).

Although classed as microlights, the Foot Launched Microlight (FLM) and Single-Seat Deregulated (SSDR) aircraft do not come under full regulation; the pilot of the former is not even required to have a licence. An SSDR microlight does not require an airworthiness document or noise certificate, but must be registered with the CAA and insured. Its pilot also has to hold a licence.

Currently we live in a state of flux as the UK moves towards a future outside the EU. It would be naive not to face the fact that there may be alterations to come – alterations that cannot be foreseen and cannot therefore be included in this edition. Should any further changes come about that directly affect you as a student pilot you should be informed at once by your instructor.

Current Definition of a Microlight

The Maximum Total Weight Authorised (MTWA) of a microlight aeroplane designed to carry not more than two persons is as follows:

450 kg for a two-seat landplane (472.5 kg if equipped with an airframe mounted total

recovery parachute system),

and

495 kg for a two-seat amphibian or float-plane;

or

300 kg for a single-seat landplane (315 kg if equipped with an airframe mounted total recovery parachute system),

and

330 kg for a single-seat amphibian or float-plane.

or

390 kg for an amateur built single-seat land-plane for which an airworthiness document was in force prior to 1st January 2003.

In addition to the MTWA limits, microlight aeroplanes must have a stall speed or minimum steady flight speed in the landing configuration not exceeding 35 knots Calibrated Airspeed. (Note: Calibrated Airspeed is broadly similar to Rectified Airspeed in the region of 35 knots).

Microlights designed to carry one person, flying on a private flight within the UK and complying with the definition of a single seat microlight are termed SSDR microlight aircraft and are not subject to formal airworthiness arrangements.

Aeroplane Airworthiness

All microlight aeroplanes, except SSDRs and FLMs, come under EASA/CAA airworthiness regulations. It is essential that you know the basics of this legislation if you intend to purchase your own machine.

Before any documentation can be processed, the aeroplane must be registered with the CAA and have the allocated letters displayed on its surfaces.

The CAA will only send an airworthiness document to the name appearing in the UK Register of Aeroplanes.

The documentation issued by the CAA does not necessarily confer the right to fly your microlight outside the UK. Before planning overseas trips you should check the requirements for the countries you intend to visit.

The BMAA are able to provide information for the most frequently visited destinations.

Since 1st April 1988, all microlight aeroplanes, except SSDRs and FLMs, must be in possession of a Noise Certificate issued by the CAA on behalf of the Department of Transport.

There are three categories of aeroplane for airworthiness purposes:

Type Approved Aeroplanes

Are all microlight aeroplanes that first flew **after** 1st January 1984.

They must have gained CAA Type Approval for their designs and the manufacturers producing them must have CAA Company Approval.

In order to fly legally, a Type Approved aeroplane must be in possession of a **Type Approved Permit to Fly** (except SSDR or FLM).

Type Accepted Aeroplanes

Are all microlight aeroplanes that first flew **prior** to 1st January 1984 if *over* 70 kg empty weight

or

prior to 1st January 1987 if *under* 70 kg empty weight.

They must have gained Type Acceptance and have a **Type Accepted Permit to Fly** to fly legally (except SSDR or FLM).

Type Accepted aeroplanes are machines that were flying before the introduction of legislation, but on investigation of their engineering, flight performance and track record, there has been sufficient evidence shown to warrant them continuing to fly subject to any necessary modification.

Amateur Built Aeroplanes

Aeroplanes constructed by the owner from scratch or from a kit require a **Type Accepted Permit to Fly** to fly legally (except SSDR or FLM).

Validation of Airworthiness Documents

Airworthiness documents are validated as follows:

Permit to Fly

Annually – subject to a satisfactory inspection by an approved Inspector and followed by a satisfactory check flight.

Inspections
Must be carried out against a laid-down schedule and any specific documents pertinent to the aeroplane type.

Check Flights
Must be carried out against a laid-down schedule and if the Permit to Fly is not valid, the check flight must be authorised by an approved inspector.

Must be carried out **within 60 days of the inspection**.

Issues
A Permit to Fly of any sort must have been validated before legal flight can take place.

Modifications
With the exception of SSDRs, no modification may be made to a microlight aeroplane **without** the approval of the CAA or a body approved by the CAA (such as the BMAA or the microlight's manufacturer).

Pilot Medical Requirements
So much for the aeroplanes; now we look at you, the pilot.

Before you can obtain a flying licence you must be in possession of a current medical declaration or medical certificate.

This document also acts as a licence for you to go solo while undergoing flight training, but you are not allowed to carry passengers on the strength of it.

Your medical fitness to fly is affirmed by the means of a self-declaration that you meet the medical standards required to hold a DVLA Group 1 Ordinary Driving Licence (ODL). You must also be able to confirm that you do not suffer from a 'disqualifying medical condition'; if you do, then you should consult an Aeromedical Examiner (AME).

The Pilot Medical Declaration is completed online at www.caa.co.uk/srg1210. The document includes full details of what would require you to consult with an AME and how to locate one.

After initial issue the validity periods of the medical declaration are as follows:

- Pilots less than 70 years of age: valid until 70 years of age
- Pilots of 70 years of age or more: valid for three years

It is your legal responsibility to ensure that you are fit to fly. You must withdraw your declaration if you no longer satisfy the requirements of the Pilot Medical Declaration or if you have been advised by a medical practitioner that you should cease flying. In order to return to flying you must consult with an AME.

National Private Pilots Licence (NPPL) (Ratings)
There are two types of rating.

Microlight

Powered Parachute

Within each type there is a further sub-division. Qualifications and limitations are as follows.

NPPL (Microlight)
Restricted With Operational Limitations
a) A minimum of 15 hours flying instruction on a microlight aeroplane of which 7 hours must be solo. The solo hours must be completed within the 24-month period prior to the date of application for a licence.

b) Pass a General Skills Test (GST) carried out by an authorised instructor holding an Flight Examiner (FE) Authority within the 9-month period prior to the date of application for a licence.

c) Pass examinations in Aeroplanes Technical, Air Law, Human Performance Limitations, Navigation and Meteorology within the 24-month period prior to the date of application for the licence.

d) Flying on a 'Restricted' rating means that you cannot fly
   - When the cloud base is below 1000 ft
   - When the in-flight visibility is below 10 km
   - Outside a radius of 8 nm from your take-off point.

e) You cannot carry passengers until you have logged at least 25 hours flight time on a microlight aeroplane, of which at least 10 hours must have been as Pilot-in-Command and your log book has been endorsed by an Examiner to verify those hours.

Unrestricted Without Operational Limitations

a) In addition to requirements a), b) and c) for the NPPL (Microlight) Restricted.

b) Obtain a further 10 hours flying time on a microlight aeroplane of which at least 5 hours must be navigation training under instructor supervision, to include 3 hours solo.

c) During the navigation training, complete 2 solo cross-country flights of at least 40 nautical miles (nm) each, over different routes.

d) During each cross-country flight an out-landing must be made at a site at least 15 nm from the take-off point.

A pilot may go straight for the Unrestricted Rating from the start, in which case the navigational cross-country requirements must also be completed within the 24-month period prior to applying for the licence.

NPPL (Powered Parachute)
Restricted With Operational Limitations

a) A minimum of 4 hours flying instruction on a powered parachute aeroplane of which at least one hour must be solo.

b) During the period of flight instruction carry out no fewer than 25 take-offs and full-stop landings of which 6 must be solo.

c) The above hours and flights must be completed within the 24-month period prior to applying for a licence.

d) Pass a General Skills Test (GST) carried out by an authorised Instructor holding an Examiner (X) appointment within the 9-month period prior to the date of application for a licence.

e) Pass examinations in Aeroplanes Technical, Air Law, Human Performance Limitations, Navigation and Meteorology within the 24-month period prior to the date of application for the licence.

f) Flying on a 'Restricted' rating means that you cannot fly

  – When the cloud base is below 1000 ft

  – When the in-flight visibility is below 10 km

  – Outside a radius of 8 nm from your take-off point

g) You cannot carry passengers until you have logged at least 15 hours flight time, of which at least 6 hours must have been as Pilot-in-Command (PIC) and your log book has been endorsed by an Examiner to verify those hours.

Unrestricted Without Operational Limitations

a) In addition to requirements a), b), c), d) and e) for the NPPL (Powered Parachute) Restricted,

b) Obtain a further 11 hours flying time on a powered parachute aeroplane, to include 5 hours solo of which at least 5 hours must be navigation training under instructor supervision, to include 3 hours solo.

c) During the navigation training, complete 2 solo cross-country flights of at least 25 nm each over different routes and sites.

d) During each cross-country flight an out-landing must be made at a site at least 10 nm from the take-off point.

A pilot may go straight for the Unrestricted rating without operational limitations from the start, in which case the solo navigational cross-country requirements must also be completed within the 24-month period prior to the date of application for a licence.

Keeping a Licence Valid

Apart from being in possession of a current declaration of fitness to keep your licence valid, there are naturally flying requirements to be fulfilled.

When flying with a passenger, who is not also a licensed microlight pilot, you must have completed 3 take-offs and landings in the previous 90 days.

Although the NPPL is valid for life, its aircraft class rating (i.e. Microlight) is only valid for 24 months. To revalidate the rating an Examiner must certify that during that period you have flown at least 12 hours, 8 of which must be as P.1 (Pilot-in-Command). In addition, you are required to have carried out at least 12 take-offs and landings and undertaken 1 hour's training with a qualified Instructor. You must also have flown at least 6 hours in the 12 months preceding the expiry date of the current certificate.

If you have not achieved the relevant experience as outlined above, you will be required to undergo a General Skills Test (GST) with an Examiner. Successful completion of this flight test, will be certified by the Examiner. If the rating has expired for more than 5 years, you will have to undergo further training, a GST and oral examination.

Privileges of the NPPL (M) or (PP) Ratings

The privileges concern the limitations under which you may fly any aeroplane within the group covered by your licence. They largely concern the rules and the flight conditions pertaining to them. In aviation as a whole these can appear to be quite complex.

However, you need only be concerned with the rules under what are called **Visual Flight Rules (VFR)** and flight conditions called **Visual Meteorological Conditions (VMC)**. As a microlight pilot, the minimum requirements for compliance with VFR are depicted in Figure 6.1. Assuming your rating is 'Unrestricted', for the majority of your flying, here in a nutshell is what you must do.

a) Always when below 3000 ft AMSL (above mean sea level):

  – be clear of cloud and in sight of the surface

  – have an in-flight visibility of not less than 1500 m

b) Always when above 3000 ft AMSL:

  – have an in-flight visibility of not less than 5 km

  – never be less than 1500 m from cloud horizontally

  – never be less than 1000 ft vertically from cloud.

Note that, all the above rules only apply **outside** controlled airspace; also, if you intend going above 10,000 ft AMSL or faster than 140 knots then the relevant rules may be found on page 92.

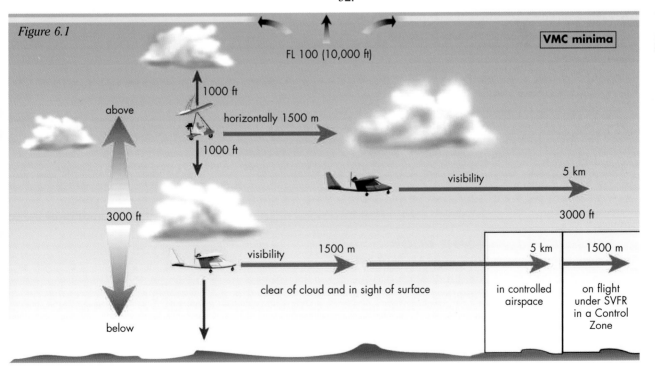

Figure 6.1

VMC minima

FL 100 (10,000 ft)

1000 ft

above

horizontally 1500 m

1000 ft

visibility 5 km

3000 ft

3000 ft

visibility 1500 m

5 km 1500 m

clear of cloud and in sight of surface

in controlled airspace

on flight under SVFR in a Control Zone

below

VMC Requirements

A word of caution: just because the minimum requirements for VMC are met, it doesn't mean that it is a good idea to go flying. During your flying training your instructor will have the opportunity to demonstrate what different weather conditions look like from both the air and the ground. In the meantime, whilst a visibility of 1500 m may permit compliance with VFR, in practice it represents very poor flying conditions.

You may have noticed that *weather* criteria is defined in a mixture of feet and metres. The main reason for this conflict is that heights are still given in feet due to the fact that most altimeters worldwide are calibrated thus.

You will also come across definitions which are in feet, kilometres and nautical miles (nm). The latter situation applies to *navigational* data relating to air traffic zones and suchlike.

Conditions Specific to Permits to Fly

A Permit to Fly (PTF) may carry any and many limitations. Prior to flying a Permit aeroplane the pilot should check the document – particularly when it is not his/her aircraft. Most microlight aircraft are restricted as follows:

- A microlight aeroplane shall not be flown for the purposes of public transport or aerial work, other than aerial work consisting solely of the giving of instruction in flying where the aeroplane is **Type Approved**.

- A microlight aeroplane is **not** permitted to perform aerobatics at any time. Steep turns not exceeding 60 degrees (unless the aeroplane manual gives a lower figure) and stalls are not considered to be aerobatic manoeuvres.

- A microlight aeroplane is not permitted to fly at night.

Personal Flying Log Book

A personal flying log book must be kept by qualified pilots or pupils under training for the purposes of becoming qualified. This log book must be kept available for producing to any recognised authority for a minimum of two years after the date of the last entry.

It must contain particulars of all flights made as a flight crew member or for the purposes of renewing a licence or rating. Flying hours count from the time the aeroplane moves off from rest under its own power for the purposes of undertaking flight to the time it comes to rest on landing and power is switched off.

The particulars to be recorded are:

- Date of flight

- Type of aircraft

- Registration letters of aircraft

- Name of Pilot-in-Command (PIC)

- Status as pilot in flight (if not PIC)

- Place/time of departure

- Place/time of arrival

- Total flight time

- Details of any particular activity, e.g. test, training, etc.

Airworthiness Log Books

Separate log books are also required to be kept in respect of both your airframe and engine; however, there is a specially approved combined log book where details of both the requirements may be kept under one cover.

All entries about incidents, inspections, maintenance, etc., must be completed in the log(s) within seven days of an occurrence – together with details of both flying and engine hours.

Radio Telephony and Transponders

As microlights have become more and more advanced in their capability to travel, so the use of radio equipment is becoming greater. One tip, do remember to call up in good time; if you don't, you may easily enter a zone or area before receiving your instructions.

The wavebands are crowded with transmissions, and this calls for accuracy and brevity in their use. A radio-equipped aircraft is deemed to be a 'radio station' and to operate one requires that you undertake a short course in procedures followed by a simple test of your competency.

On successful completion of the course you will be issued with a **Flight Radio Telephony Operator's Licence**.

Whilst the primary radar used by air traffic controllers does not utilise airborne equipment, Secondary Surveillance Radar (SSR) requires that an aircraft is equipped with a transponder. The fitting of a transponder is becoming more common place due to the increasing reliance that is placed on the information provided by these units. A transponder is a device that responds with data that allows, as a minimum and dependent upon mode, the aircraft's position to be determined. This information may also be used by other aircraft that are equipped with an Airborne Collision Avoidance System (ACAS).

When a transponder is interrogated it transmits or 'Squawks' a coded 4 digit signal assigned by an air traffic controller and selected by the pilot. For identification purposes the transponder is equipped with an 'IDENT' function that, when selected, produces an enhanced transmission. Frequency Monitoring, Conspicuity and Special Purpose Codes, each with a specific meaning, are used when not receiving an air traffic service or to indicate a condition. For example, the code 7000 is used for conspicuity, whilst 7700 indicates an emergency condition. The use of a transponder is mandatory above FL100 (10,000 feet).

An Aircraft Radio Licence is required for all radio equipment. The licence can be obtained from the CAA Agency for either a fixed installation or an 'aircraft transportable licence' for a handheld, which can be used in any aeroplane. The price is the same for each.

UK Airspace
Airspace in the UK below Flight Level (FL) 245 (24,500 ft) is divided into two **Flight Information Regions (FIRs)** known as the **London FIR** and the **Scottish FIR**.

Above FL245 the same regions are known as **Upper Flight Information Regions (UFIRs)**.

All airspace is either controlled or uncontrolled. It is further divided into classes of airspace – each with its own set of flight requirements. In controlled airspace there are to be found zones and areas as follows.

Zones and Areas
Control Zone (CTR)
Defined airspace from the surface to a specified altitude (QNH) or flight level (FL).

Control Area (CTA)
Defined airspace extending upwards from a specified altitude (QNH) or flight level (FL) to an upper limit expressed as a flight level.

Airway
A control area in the form of a corridor which extends 5 nm either side of a line joining two places at which navigational aids are usually sited.

Each airway has specified vertical limits and has its own letter/number identification code.

Terminal Manoeuvring Area (TMA)
Is similar to a CTA, but is the name given to some large control areas around selected major aerodromes – for example, the London TMA (LTMA).

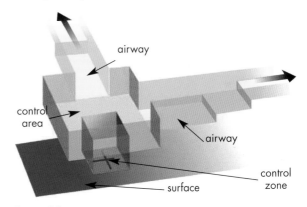

Figure 6.2

Radio and Transponder Mandatory Zones
Radio Mandatory Zone (RMZ)
Defined airspace inside which it is necessary to establish two way voice communications with the controlling authority. Entry without fulfilling this requirement may be possible by local agreement.

Transponder Mandatory Zone (TMZ)

Defined airspace inside which the carriage and use of a transponder is a requirement. Entry without fulfilling this requirement may be possible with the permission of the controlling authority.

Classes of Airspace

Controlled
Class A
Airways and certain defined CTAs and TMAs

Class B
Not allocated in the UK at present

Class C
Mainly airspace above FL195

Class D
Defined CTRs and CTAs

Class E
As and when defined, for example:

- Parts of the Scottish TMA at and below 6000 feet AMSL

- The Belfast TMA

- Certain airways.

Uncontrolled
Class F
Not allocated in the UK at present.

Class G
Open airspace

The above classes are depicted on UK aeronautical charts as follows:

Class A ——————————————

Class C —— —— — —— — —— —

Class D —— —— —— —— —— ——

Class E —— —— —— —— —— ——

Class G ⊥——⊥——⊥——⊥——⊥——⊥

(As and when allocated:)

Class B —— — —— — —— — ——

Class F —— — —— — —— — ——

Note: The above identification markings for airspace are different on the charts of other European States; as yet there is no agreed ICAO standard.

We will now go on to deal with the rules for flying within these classes of airspace and the minimum weather criteria attached to them. Again, these rules are in compliance with agreement reached with the ICAO.

You will recall that inside controlled airspace there can be zones and areas which are 'notified' and for which the rules will be different.

Special VFR Flight (SVFR)

A SVFR clearance may be issued by an Air Traffic Control (ATC) unit to allow flight in a Control Zone when VMC does not prevail. At all times, however, you must operate within the limitations of your licence.

> Diverting for a moment, there are additional qualifications where other pilots can operate to lower limits than yourself, such as flying in cloud, or poor visibility, in what are known as **Instrument Meteorological Conditions (IMC)** under **Instrument Flight Rules (IFR)**. To fly in IMC under IFR a pilot requires an **IMC rating** or an **Instrument Rating (IR)**.
>
> There is the **Night Rating** for flying at night (obviously!), with night being defined as between half an hour after sunset to half an hour before sunrise. Sunset and sunrise are defined as being seen at the surface – not from the air. You should recall that a microlight is not permitted to fly at night.
>
> Currently no microlight licence can have any of the above ratings attached to it. Perhaps you can see why this chapter is confining itself in the main only to what you need to know!

A SVFR clearance requires that an aircraft remains clear of cloud, at an airspeed of less than 140 knots and with a minimum visibility of 1500 m.

Should the authorised route make the rule of maintaining 1000 ft above the highest fixed object within 600 m impossible to obey, then you are absolved from complying with it.

However, do bear in mind that authorisation you may be given does not absolve you from the obligation to be able to 'land clear' as laid down in b) under 'Low Flying Rules'. (See page 78.)

Flight Plans

A flight plan consists of details of a planned flight, which is lodged with ATC not less than 60 minutes prior to departure for VFR flight. ATC then notify all concerned, but will still require the PIC to 'book out' on leaving.

Flight plans are usually associated with commercial or IFR flights, but a private pilot may file one and in fact is definitely advised to do so if intending to fly more than 10 nm off the coast or over mountainous or sparsely populated areas.

Should you be over 30 minutes overdue at your destination, or land at an airfield other than your original destination without informing the latter, then a search and rescue operation will be set in motion.

Should your point of departure and/or arrival not have a fully equipped Air Traffic Control (ATC) facility, it will be necessary for alternative arrangements to be made as a notification of take-off and landing must be made to ATC. If a flight is planned to a destination without ATC it is imperative that a 'responsible person' is aware of the aircraft's ETA and will therefore be able to contact ATC if overdue action is required.

A flight plan is mandatory if you intend to cross an international boundary.

Guidance for the completion and submission of flight plans is provided in CAA Publication CAP 694; the document is accessible via the CAA's website, www.caa.co.uk.

Pre-Flight Actions

The PIC must always ensure that all conditions in relation to the aeroplane and the planned flight are correct in every way and, in case of an emergency, the passengers are aware of what to do and the location of safety equipment.

Aerodrome Traffic Zones – Civil and Military

Many aerodromes lie outside controlled airspace, but this does not mean there is no form of procedure. Most of them have their own zones as follows.

Aerodrome Traffic Zone (ATZ)

Extends up to 2000 ft above aerodrome level (QFE) and outwards within a radius of 2 nm centred on the mid-point of the longest runway, where the runway length is less than 1850 m. Otherwise, it is 2.5 nm.

On no account should entry into an ATZ with an air traffic control unit be made without prior permission given over the radio or by telephone prior to flight.

On permission being granted, if you are flying non-radio, keep a sharp look-out for visual signals in the signals area and for light signals, which can come from the control tower or a caravan placed near the take-off point on the runway in use.

If you are equipped with radio and just passing through an ATZ, you should report your position and height on entering and leaving the zone.

It is essential to be fully aware of an aerodrome's requirements before flying in.

Civil aerodrome ATZs are active during published hours of operation. Military and Governmnent aerodrome ATZs are active at notified times.

Military Aerodrome Traffic Zone (MATZ)

Extended ATZ reaching up to 3000 ft above aerodrome level (QFE) within 5 nm radius of the centre of the aerodrome.

A MATZ can sometimes have a 'stub' or 'Panhandle' projecting from the circle extending from 1000 ft to 3000 ft above ground level (QFE) being 4 nm in width and 5 nm in length.

Some military aerodromes are shown on charts devoid of any MATZ marking. Also, the MATZ itself has no mandatory power.

However, penetration of a MATZ without contacting ATC would be foolhardy in view of the nature of the flying that can take place from such airfields – and anyway the ATZ rules still stand.

Military Low Flying

There are areas in the UK where military low flying can take place up to 2000 ft AGL, although such activity is usually between 250 and 500 ft AGL. Such areas are not under any control, so there is a particular need to keep a careful look-out at all times.

General Flight Rules

Just as you have the 'highway code' for motoring, so in the air there are rules and signals that have to be obeyed.

A 'flight' is designated to be from engine on to engine off. These rules extend to movement on the ground as well.

Reference will occasionally be made to the term 'flying machine'. This is the official description of a power-driven, heavier-than-air aircraft.

One point you must remember is that whatever the rules may say, it is the PIC who is responsible for avoiding a collision when all is said and done. This philosophy also applies regardless of any ATC clearance given.

Low Flying Rules

The public very soon notice a low flying aircraft and their reaction has considerable bearing on the image of the pilot and of flying itself.

The pertinent rules are as follows

a) An aircraft shall not fly closer than 500 ft to any person, vessel, vehicle or structure.

   Exceptions to this rule are:

   – Taking off and landing

   – Gliders while slope soaring

   – Performance at an aircraft race, contest or display where the appropriate permission has been obtained.

Do note that the 500 ft rule is not a height stipulation, it is a 'distance from' rule. This is often misunderstood, particularly by the public when complaining.

b) An aircraft other than a helicopter shall not fly over a congested area such as a city, town or settlement used mainly for residential, industrial, commercial or recreational purposes

   – below a height that would allow it to land clear of the area without danger to people or property in the event of engine failure

   or

   – at less than 1000 ft above the highest fixed object within a horizontal distance of 600m,

   Exceptions to this rule are:

   – Taking off and landing

   – Flying on an authorised SVFR flight

c) At an open-air assembly of more than 1000 people no aircraft shall fly:

   – Over that assembly at a height below 1000 ft, or

   – At such height as will permit, in the event of a power unit failure, the aircraft to alight clear of the assembly

   whichever is the higher

In addition an aircraft shall not land or take-off within 1000 m of an organised open-air assembly of more than 1000 persons unless at an aerodrome in accordance with approved procedures.

The exception to this is:
– At a landing site other than an aerodrome when flying with the appropriate permission of the authority and organiser of the event.

Again you should have deduced that while these are the general rules, you still have limitations attached to your Permit to Fly that cannot be ignored.

However, all rules go out the window when action is necessary for the saving of life.

Collision Avoidance and Rights of Way

En Route
– Flying machines must give way to airships, gliders and balloons.

– Airships must give way to gliders and balloons.

– Gliders must give way to balloons.

– An aircraft giving way must avoid passing over, under or crossing ahead of the other aircraft until well clear of it.

- When two aircraft are converging at about the same altitude, the aircraft that has the other on its right must give way (Figure 6.3).

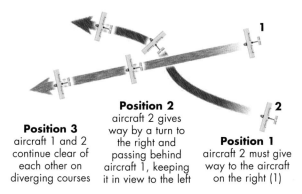

Position 3
aircraft 1 and 2 continue clear of each other on diverging courses

Position 2
aircraft 2 gives way by a turn to the right and passing behind aircraft 1, keeping it in view to the left

Position 1
aircraft 2 must give way to the aircraft on the right (1)

Figure 6.3 Approaching on converging courses

Notes:
- Should the aircraft to the left be towing another aircraft or an object such as a banner, then the one on the right must give way.

- In all other respects a flying machine towing another aircraft shall be considered to be a single aircraft under the command of the pilot of the towing aircraft.

- When two aircraft are approaching head-on, or nearly so, each must turn right (Figure 6.4)

Figure 6.4 When approaching head on, each aircraft turns right

- An aircraft with right-of-way should maintain course and speed.

- An aircraft must not fly so close to other aircraft as to create a danger of collision.

- An aircraft overtaking another aircraft shall turn to the right (Figure 6.5).

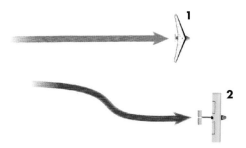

Figure 6.5 When overtaking another aircraft, the overtaking aircraft turns right

Notes:
- This applies whether climbing or descending as well as in level flight.

- A glider, however, may turn right or left.

- An aircraft following a prominent landmark such as a railway, motorway, coastline and so forth should keep such a landmark to its left (Figure 6.6).

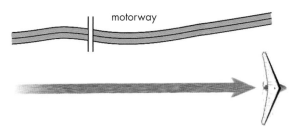

Figure 6.6 When following a main ground feature, the feature is kept on the left

Near an Aerodrome
- An aircraft approaching or flying in the vicinity of an aerodrome must conform to the pattern of traffic formed by other aircraft intending to land there.

Note:
- If unable to do so the aircraft should keep well clear of the airspace in which the pattern is formed.

- All turns should be made to the left unless ground signals state otherwise.

- An aircraft landing or on final approach has right of way over others in flight or on the ground.

- Where two or more aircraft of similar category (e.g. two flying machines) are approaching to land, the lower aircraft has right of way.

Note:

- The lower aircraft must not be cutting in or overtaking another at the time.

- When ATC has given an aircraft a place in the priority for landing, this sequence must be adhered to.

- When an aircraft commander is aware that another is making an emergency landing, he must give way.

  Note:

  - If this should occur at night he must await further permission to land irrespective of any earlier directions given.

Take-off and Landing

- Take-off must be in the direction indicated by ground signals.

- Landing on a runway that is occupied by other aircraft must not take place unless authorised by ATC.

- Where take-offs and landings are not confined to a runway, an aircraft that is landing must leave clear on its left any aircraft that has landed or is landing or is about to take-off.

  Note:

  - Any turn must be to the left as long as there is no interference with other traffic.

- A flying machine about to take off must manoeuvre so as to leave clear on its left any aircraft that has already taken off or is about to do so.

- A flying machine on landing must move clear of the landing area as soon as possible unless ATC says otherwise.

- There are rules about landing and take-off in respect of wake turbulence caused by other aircraft. The official figures are to be found in Chapter 8 Meteorology on page 120.

On the Ground

- Aircraft on the ground must give way to those taking off or landing.

- Vehicles towing aircraft must give way to aircraft.

- Vehicles must give way to vehicles towing aircraft.

  Note:

  - The above are in order of priority.

- When two aircraft are taxiing towards each other head-on, or nearly so, each must turn to the right.

- When two aircraft are converging, the one that has the other on its right must give way – avoiding crossing ahead of the other unless passing well clear.

- An aircraft overtaking another aircraft or vehicle may turn left or right and must keep well clear.

Signals

When no radio is carried the Air Traffic Controller will communicate with the aircraft using visual signals.

These signals fall into two broad categories – general and particular.

General signals are those applicable to all users of the aerodrome in question and are to be seen laid out in a 40 ft by 40 ft hollow white square known as the 'Signals Area'. Signals in this area should be easily readable by a pilot flying over at 2000 ft and are covered later in this section.

Particular signals are those that are specific to an individual aircraft at a given time. Normally they are made by coloured beams of light emitted from an 'Aldis' type lamp. There are occasions when star shells will be used, fired by a Very pistol.

Signals to an Aircraft on the Ground

Intermittent Green Beam – You may move on the manoeuvring area and apron.

Continuous Green Beam – You may take off.

Intermittent Red Beam – Move clear of landing area.

Continuous Red Beam – Stop.

Intermittent White Beam – Return to starting point on aerodrome.

Signals to an Aircraft in the Air

Intermittent Green Beam – Return to aerodrome – wait for permission to land.

Continuous Green Beam – You may land.

Intermittent Red Beam – Do not land – aerodrome not available for landing.

Continuous Red Beam – Give way to other aircraft and continue circling.

Intermittent White Beam – Land at this aerodrome after receiving continuous green and after intermittent green proceed to apron.

Red Pyrotechnic or Flare – Do not land – wait for permission.

Signals from an Aircraft in the Air to an Aerodrome

Red Pyrotechnic or Flare – Immediate assistance is requested.

Continuous or Intermittent Green Beam or Green Pyrotechnic – By night: may I land? – By day: may I land in a different direction to the landing 'T'?

Intermittent White Beam *or* **White Pyrotechnic lights** *or* **switching navigation or landing lights on and off** – I am compelled to land.

Ground Signals at Aerodromes

With the prevalence of radio, some aerodromes have abandoned their signal squares. However, many remain in use.

The following are some of the signals that you will come across.

Landing prohibited

– A **red** square panel with **yellow** diagonals denotes the aerodrome is unsafe and landing there is prohibited. (Fig 6.7).

Figure 6.7

Special Precautions

– A **red** square panel with one **yellow** diagonal denotes that the manoeuvring area is poor and special care is needed when landing.

Figure 6.8

Use Hard Surfaces at All Times

– A **white** dumb-bell denotes that the movement of aeroplanes and gliders on the ground is confined to hard surfaces only.

Figure 6.9

Use Only Hard Surfaces for Take-off and Landing

– A **white** dumb-bell with **black** strips at right angles to the shaft denotes taking off and landing shall be on hard surfaces, but ground movement is not so restricted.

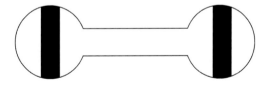

Figure 6.10

Right-hand Circuit

– A **Red** and **yellow** striped arrow along two sides of the signal area and pointing clockwise denotes a right-hand circuit is in force (Figure 6.11).

Figure 6.11

Direction of Take-off and Landing

– A **white** or **orange** 'T' denotes the direction of take-off and landing should be parallel to the shaft and towards the cross arm.

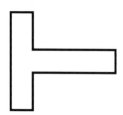

Figure 6.12

Gliding

– A double **white** cross denotes that gliding is in progress.

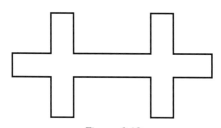

Figure 6.13

Runway Indication

– Two-figure **black** numerals on a **yellow** background denote the runway in use.

Figure 6.14

Reporting Point

– A **black** 'C' on a **yellow** background denotes this point.

Figure 6.15

Surface Markings at Aerodromes

Aerodromes display a wide variety of surface markings to indicate the layout of runways and taxiways. In addition, areas reserved for specialist activities or areas to be avoided are identified by markers.

Aerodrome markings range from simple chalk lines on a grass airfield to the complexities of signs, lights and markings associated with international airports.

The following figures highlight some of the markings that you may come across as a microlight pilot.

Runways are always demarked with white markings, whilst taxiways are identified with yellow markings.

Boundaries

– Markers/Flags with **orange/white** stripes are used to mark boundaries of unfit areas. They can also indicate aerodrome boundaries.

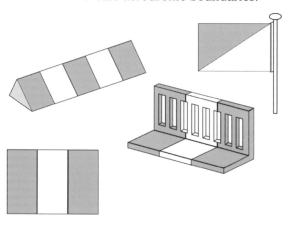

Figure 6.16

Helicopter Operations

- A **white** letter 'H' indicates an area which must be used only for helicopters taking off and landing.

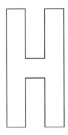

Figure 6.17

Picking Up and Dropping of Cables

- A **yellow** cross denotes the area for the picking up and dropping of tow ropes, banners, etc.

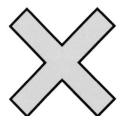

Figure 6.18

Direction of Taking Off and Landing

- A **white** 'T' placed at the left-hand side of a runway (when viewed from the direction of landing) indicates the runway (or direction, if no runway) to be used for take-off and landing.

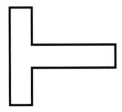

Figure 6.19

Unserviceable Portion of Runway/Taxiway

- Two or more **white** (runway) or **yellow** (taxiway) crosses at 45° to the centre line and not more than 300 metres apart denote the section so marked as unfit for aircraft movement.

Figure 6.20

Runway Holding Positions

- Two broken yellow lines and two solid yellow lines denote the position on a taxiway beyond which Air Traffic Control (ATC) clearance is required before entering the runway. If there is no ATC then the runway must be clear of aircraft taking off and landing before proceeding.

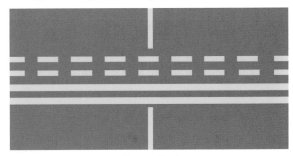

Figure 6.21

- Two solid yellow lines connected with yellow perpendicular lines denote a holding position, other than that closest to the runway (see Fig 6.21), beyond which ATC clearance is required before proceeding towards the runway. If there is no ATC then the markings may be disregarded.

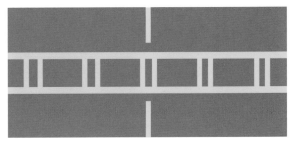

Figure 6.22

As microlights become more readily accepted at aerodromes, there are additional signs to be taken into consideration.

Marshalling Signals from Marshal to Pilot for Fixed Wing Aeroplanes

See Table 6.1 on page 85.

Distress Signals

For an aircraft in grave or imminent danger needing immediate help or in a situation likely to lead to same

- Over radio telephone (RT):

  • The call sign 'Mayday' is given out three times on the frequency in use or on 121.5 MHz

- Visually:

  • SOS in Morse

  • Succession of single red pyrotechnics at short intervals

  • A red parachute flare

- Sound (other than RT):

  • Continuous sound made by any means.

For an aircraft in difficulties that compel it to land, but not in need of immediate help, where no RT is available:

- Succession of white pyrotechnics

- Repeated switching on and off of landing lights

- Repeated switching on and off of navigation lights in a manner different to normal flashing lights if this type is fitted.

Where an urgent message needs to be sent concerning the safety of, say, a ship, aircraft, vehicle, property or person within sight of the aircraft:

- Over RT: 'PAN' is given out six times on the frequency in use or on 121.5 MHz

- Visually: XXX in Morse

- Sound (other than RT): XXX in Morse

Navigation Lights

At night flying machines and airships display navigation lights at each side that show through 110° from dead ahead – red on the port (left) and green on the starboard (right) side. At the tail a single white light shows through 140° when viewed from dead astern – 70° on either side (Figure 6.23).

As you can see, one of the lights is visible at all times as the spread covers 360°.

Careful note of a navigation light and its bearing from you will help to avoid a collision at night.

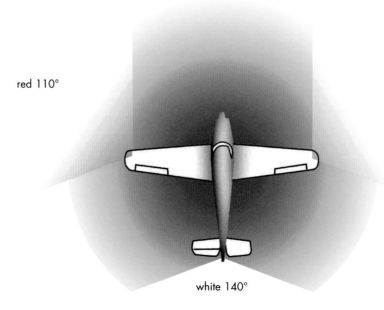

red 110°   green 110°

white 140°

Figure 6.23

Table 6.1 Marshalling Signals

Signal	Description	Meaning
Figure 6.24	 Right or left arm down. Other arm moved across body and extended to position of other marshal	Proceed to guidance from another marshal
Figure 6.25	 Arms repeatedly moved upward and backward beckoning onward	Move ahead
Figure 6.26	 Right arm down, left arm repeatedly moved upward and backward. Speed of movement indicates rate of turn	Turn to port (left) or open up starboard engine
Figure 6.27	 Left arm down, right arm repeatedly moved upward and backward. Speed of movement indicates rate of turn	Turn to starboard (right) or open up port engine
Figure 6.28	 Arms repeatedly crossed above the head. Speed of movement denotes urgency required	Stop
Figure 6.29	 Circular motion of the right hand at head level with the left arm pointing to the appropriate engine	Start engine
Figure 6.30	 Arms extended, the palms facing then swung from the extended position inwards	Chocks inserted
Figure 6.31	 Arms down, the palms facing outwards then swung outwards	Chocks away
Figure 6.32	 Either arm and hand placed level with the chest. Then moved laterally with the palm downward	Cut engine
Figure 6.33	 Arms placed down, with the palms towards the ground then moved up and down several times	Slow down
Figure 6.34	 Arms placed down, with the palms towards the ground, then either the right or left arm moved up and down indicating that the motors on the left or right side, as the case may be, should be slowed down	Slow down engine(s) on side indicated
Figure 6.35	 Arms placed above the head in a vertical position	This bay or parking spot
Figure 6.36	 Right arm raised at the elbow with the palm facing forward	All clear – marshalling is completed

Diagrammatically it is difficult to provide examples of how to assess clear or collision situations as, movement on the part of two objects is involved.

A useful exercise can be to cut out aircraft outlines from card or paper and with a protractor accurately mark out the respective lights – colouring them in when finished.

In moving the models about you will see for yourself which lights are visible and their bearings in relation to whether a potential collision situation exists or not. A useful tip is this: if there is no change in the bearing of another aircraft then a potential collision situation exists.

If any required light should fail in flight, the aircraft must land as soon as it is safe to do so unless authorised to continue by ATC.

A glider does not necessarily have to display full navigational lights as just discussed. It has the option to do as free balloons do and that is to display a steady red light visible in all
directions.

An anti-collision light when carried on any aircraft is a flashing red light showing in all directions.

Air Light Beacons

Air light beacons are installed at various civil and military aerodromes in the UK. They come in two forms.

Identification beacons

– These flash a two-letter Morse group every 12 seconds: Green at civil aerodromes, red at military aerodromes.

Aerodrome beacons

– An alternating colour flash signal, usually white/green.

Beacons normally operate at night and during the day if the visibility is bad.

Restrictions and Obstructions in Airspace

There are areas over which flight may be restricted or prohibited either temporarily or permanently.

These permanent areas are to be found outlined on aviation charts together with their vertical extent. For example: D.308/25 on a chart indicates 'Danger area No. 308' up to 25,000 ft within the area outlined. Also, the manner in which it is outlined will give an indication of the times of operation.

Permanent areas are to be found on aviation charts; for example, 'Danger Areas'. There are also such events as Royal Flights, Red Arrows displays, etc. These are promulgated by the Aeronautical Information Service (see page 87).

Obstructions are shown when they are 300 ft and over; an example is a TV mast or similar form of obstruction reaching up to an abnormal height in relation to its environment. Such structures are lit if 150 m (492 ft) or more above ground level (AGL). Between 300 ft and 150 m AGL they may be lit. Such an obstruction will be designated by a specified symbol with two sets of figures – one is the height above ground level (QFE), the other is the altitude above mean sea level (QNH).

Always take care that you read these heights in accordance with your situation at the time – the difference can be quite substantial and therefore potentially hazardous.

Aeronautical Charts

To the light aeroplane or microlight pilot, a full understanding of all types of airspace is a prerequisite to enjoying the freedom of the sky. At times you may feel intimidated by the plethora of rules and procedures, but knowledge is the key to simplifying UK airspace.

Your best guide is the standard ICAO half-million or quarter-million aeronautical chart, which not only highlights the 'no-go' areas, but the 'Reference to Air Information' section at the foot of the chart will teach you a great deal about the various types of airspace.

Such a chart should be definitely part of your reading alongside this book.

From time to time chart data can change. For operational use always ensure that you have an up-to-date issue.

Reprints take place approximately every twelve months, but changes can occur in between so reference should be made to the chart amendment service.

Note: You are under obligation in flight to be in possession of an up-to-date chart at all times. Most microlight pilots use the quarter-million map.

Aeronautical Information Service (AIS)

Previously known to many as the UK Air Pilot (UK AIP), the official publication is now referred to as the **Integrated Aeronautical Information Package**, in which not only is the UK AIP embraced (including Amendment services), but a number of other sources of information, such as:

– AIP Supplements

– Aeronautical Information Circulars (AIC)

– Notices to Airmen (Notams)

– AIS Information Line

In practice, the items in the AIP of interest to a pilot are available in **Flight Guides** obtainable from aeronautical shops. Any changes in this information will be summarised in amendments to Flight Guides together with Notams. Pilots should review AICs at regular intervals.

AICs are usually concerned with administrative matters, but may give advance notice or amplification to operational issues or matters of safety. AICs are normally issued in batches every 28 days and are colour coded according to subject matter.

Internet access to the full Integrated Aeronautical Information Package is provided by National Air Traffic Services, (NATS) at www.ais.org
The AIS Information Line telephone numbers are: 0808 5354802 or 01489 887515.

Aerodrome Traffic Services
Air Traffic Control (ATC) is responsible for the control of all aircraft in the vicinity of the aerodrome and in the manoeuvring area. From a radio point of view, a pilot starting up and taking off contacts the aerodrome 'tower' frequency. The pilot inward bound would first use the aerodrome 'approach' frequency and would be handed over to the 'tower' as and when appropriate.

Aerodrome Flight Information Service (AFIS) is provided when no ATC is available. This service cannot give instructions or advice to pilots in the air and the suffix 'information' is used in any transmissions. An AFIS unit may, however, issue instructions to aircraft on the ground.

Air/Ground Radio Station facilities can exist where no ATC or AFIS is available and such stations may be manned by people without ATC qualifications. To make it clear that no ATC or AFIS are available, the suffix 'radio' is used in any transmissions.

The UK Flight Information Services
Air Traffic Controllers are able to offer assistance outside controlled airspace to participating pilots by use of radio communication. In accepting a service from ATC the pilot reaches an accord with the controller and it is necessary for both parties to be aware of their responsibilities. In addition to the Alerting (Emergency) Service, provided whenever a controller considers it necessary; there are four types of services that pilots may request.

Basic Service
This is a non-radar service and the controller will only supply general information concerning airfield conditions, weather and airspace activity.

Procedural Service
Again this is a non-radar service provided for participating aircraft by a controller providing separation between aircraft by means of track, level and timing instructions.

Traffic service
This is a radar service and the controller will supply information concerning conflicting traffic, but no avoiding action will be offered.

Deconfliction Service
Again this is a radar service and as suggested by the name the controller will issue advisory instructions, if required, to avoid a confliction with other traffic.

Documents Carried in Flight
Should you travel overseas outside the UK – other than the Channel Islands or the Isle of Man – you must carry the following documents:

- The licence for any radio installation you may have on board.
- The aircraft's C of A or relevant airworthiness document.
- Your pilot's licence.
- Copy of Interception Procedures.
- The aircraft's registration certificate.

Again, do check your airworthiness document in relation to the aircraft being permitted to operate outside the UK.

Production of Documents
An authorised person such as a police officer, a CAA enforcement officer or any other person designated by the Secretary of State can ask you to produce documents.

These documents are:

- Your pilot's licence
- Your personal flying log book
- The aircraft's registration certificate
- The aircraft's airworthiness documentation

Note:
Your personal flying log book must be kept for production when asked for two years after the date of the last entry.

Flying at Displays
Procedures for participating in flying displays are laid down in CAA Publication CAP 403. It is important to remember that if you are to perform at a Flying Display that is open to the public, then you will need to be in possession of a Display Pilot Authorisation issued by the CAA.

Displays held at Ministry of Defence establishments do not come under CAP 403 procedures, but the organisers of flying displays at such locations will invariably require evidence of pilot competence such as a Display Pilot Authorisation issued by the CAA.

Microlight Aircraft Events that are organised by, or in association with, the BMAA are subject to arrangements contained in Chapter 7 of CAP 403. Guidance is provided for all aspects of organizing and participating in such events. CAP 403 is accessible via the CAA's website, www.caa.co.uk.

The simple act of flying into and out of an event as a visitor does not come under the regulations laid down for displays, although special arrangements may be stipulated by the organiser.

Before accepting an invitation or seeking to take part in any public event, you should contact the CAA to see where you stand. The address is – Civil Aviation Authority, Safety Regulation Group, Flight Operations Inspectorate (General Aviation) (FOI (GA)), Aviation House, Gatwick Airport South, West Sussex, RH6 0YR and the telephone number is 01293 573510/573525.

Notifiable Accidents
An accident must be notified if it is serious and happens from the time anyone, pilot or passengers, boards an aircraft with the intention of flying until such time as everybody has left that aircraft.

A serious accident is defined as:

- Anyone killed or seriously injured while in the aircraft or in direct contact with it.

or

- The aircraft suffers damage or structural failure that can affect its structural strength, performance or flight characteristics to the extent it needs major repairs.

or

– The aircraft is missing or completely inaccessible.

Note:
Exceptions to damage are engine failure or engine accessories and are limited to these alone.

– Also excepted is damage to propellers, wing tips, tyres, brakes, fairings or small dents and punctures to skin.

When a notifiable accident occurs, the aircraft commander **Pilot-in-Command (PIC)**, must notify the Chief Inspector of the Department of Transport, Air Accident Investigation Branch (AAIB) by the quickest possible means. Where the PIC is not in a position to do so, the report should be made by any other responsible person.

If the notifiable accident occurs in the UK, the local police authority must also be notified.

All accidents/incidents, **however small**, must be entered in the aeroplane's engine and airframe log book/s before the aeroplane is flown again or before the end of the day – whichever is the earlier.

Airprox Reporting Procedure

An Airprox is investigated by the UK Airprox Board (UKAB) formed by both the CAA and the Ministry of Defence (MOD).

If you consider that you have been endangered by the close proximity of another aircraft, you should radio a report at once to the nearest Air Traffic Service Unit (ATSU).

If this is not possible the report should be made by telephone or any other means to any ATSU or preferably to the Air Traffic Control Centre immediately on landing. You can also report directly to the UKAB. All reports, however made, should be confirmed within 7 days on the appropriate CAA form.

Dropping of Articles from the Air

Other than the dropping of glider tow ropes and banners at permitted sites, no person or article may be dropped from an aircraft without prior permission from the CAA.

Registration of Aircraft

All aircraft in the UK with the exception of FLMs, gliders and hang gliders must be registered with the CAA.

Registration letters of a stated size must be painted or affixed to the wings and fuselage of the aircraft.

The CAA must be notified of any change of ownership or additional ownership that takes place on an aircraft. To the Authority, it is the name that appears in the UK Register that they consider to be the person responsible even if that person has disposed of the aircraft.

Incidents

A good pilot never stops learning, and one of the finest ways to do so is by one's own mistakes and those of others.

Within the flying world there are organisations that collect and publish anonymously reports of incidents that are not necessarily serious accidents, but from which others can learn to avoid similar situations.

For example, an aeroplane owner on preflighting his machine may discover a hair-line crack in the structure. Memories sneak back of a previous heavy landing that 'fortunately' no one else had seen. Pride overwhelms conscience and the part is replaced with no report ever being made of the incident.

Suppose an identical situation had happened to other pilots? If each had submitted an incident report, a pattern would have emerged and a warning issued to owners of similar aeroplanes as to what could happen.

In doing so it is in no way trite to say that a life may be saved. Reading an accident report later and being able to say 'that fault happened on my machine, but I kept quiet' would not be a pleasant situation to live with.

Many incidents may not be reportable to the appropriate authorities, but they are certainly bound to be reported in the aircraft's engine/airframe log book to alert the inspector. In fact if the aeroplane is not immediately and safely flyable, it must be grounded and any repairs officially inspected and passed as satisfactory before further flight can take place.

Do remember, incident reports are anonymous when passed on to others, so help those others. Not to do so is the mark of a very irresponsible pilot.

Alcohol and Drugs

The ANO states that members of an aircraft's crew shall not be under the influence of drink or drugs to such as extent as to impair their capacity. The Railways and Transport Safety Act 2003 details the maximum blood alcohol limits applicable to those involved in aviation activities. The Alcohol, Medication and Drugs of Addiction section in Chapter 7, Human Performance Limitations (page 99) explains what these regulations mean to a pilot.

It is illegal for *anyone*, not just the crew, to board an aircraft when drunk.

Commercial Use of Microlights

The commercial use of any aeroplane for hire and reward, where money or goods in kind change hands for services rendered, is strictly speaking only allowed when the pilot has a Commercial Pilot's Licence (CPL).

Currently there is no microlight CPL in existence, so you are unable to undertake any flying that can be termed commercial. There is however a dispensation in that a microlight pilot with an Instructor Rating in his/her licence can be paid for their services, but only for the purposes of flight training.

Furthermore, the aeroplane used for such training must be Type Approved except in special circumstances (see below). Although complicated, without this dispensation microlight flying could well have disappeared.

Other Aspects of Hire and Reward

The law is quite complex and other areas are involved which because money can change hands the activities are deemed to be commercial – or illegal because the aeroplane does not meet a required airworthiness standard.

Once you have obtained your pilot's licence, you can hire a microlight from a club provided that it is a 'Type Approved Aeroplane'.

Should you decide to become a sole or part owner of an aircraft with a Type Accepted Permit to Fly (e.g. amateur built), it is possible for flight training and testing to take place. The flight training may be for the initial grant of a licence or rating as well as for the purposes of 'difference', 'recency' or 'revalidation'.

Again, not so long ago, it was illegal to share the costs of flying in that a passenger could not contribute towards the expenses incurred by the flight where the pilot did not hold a CPL. This has now been relaxed and a private pilot may accept a contribution towards the direct costs of the flight. There is no restriction to the proportion of the direct flight costs that the passenger may pay, but the pilot must contribute something and cannot make a profit.

Charity Flights

This is one sphere of activity that has become very popular in recent years.

Money may be raised for charities in a microlight aeroplane or powered parachute provided that a pilot flying a sponsored flight receives no payment for that flight.

A pilot may offer a flight as a prize to the winner of a competition organised by a registered charity. The CAA has produced a document for pilots wishing to offer such flights. Given the responsibilities resulting from offering a member of the public a recreational flight, the CAA's 'Charity Flight Guidance' should be considered essential reading.

The Skyway Code

The CAA General aviation Unit produces a guide called *The Skyway Code* with the intention of providing pilots with guidance on the operational, safety and regulatory issues relevant to their flying.

Whilst as a microlight pilot just about to spread their wings the scope of the Skyway

Code may appear rather daunting, it includes some practical guidance on how Air Law applies to your flying. As always, your instructor will be able to highlight the areas that are relevant to you as a microlight pilot.

Further information on how to access the Skyway Code is available from:

www.caa.co.uk/skywaycode.

Operation of Foot-Launched Microlights

Introduction

As previously mentioned in Chapter 3, Foot Launched Microlights (FLMs) are officially referred to as Self-Propelled Hang Gliders (SPHGs) and this term encompasses all types of machines capable of being foot launched, including paramotors.

A SPHG is defined by the ANO as an aircraft with an aerofoil wing and an engine that has the following features:

(a) If foot launched, has a stall speed or minimum steady flight speed in the landing configuration not exceeding 35 knots calibrated airspeed; or

(b) If wheel launched, has a stall speed or minimum steady flight speed in the landing configuration not exceeding 20 knots calibrated airspeed; and

(c) Has a maximum empty weight, including full fuel, of 70 kg, or 75 kg if wheel launched and equipped with an emergency parachute recovery system.

Additionally, the ANO categorises the SPHG as a glider for the purposes of Air Law. Broadly speaking, in flight the pilot of a SPHG is subject to the same rules as the microlight pilot, and in the case of a wheel launched aircraft, insurance is required.

Although no licence is required and therefore no examinations have to be taken, the BMAA and the BHPA (British Hang-gliding and Para-gliding Association) have initiated simple test papers linked to the rules of the air to which they will have to comply. In fact, it should be stressed that, in spite of the absence of the need for a licence, anyone attempting to fly a FLM without expert tuition would be very foolish.

As all FLM pilots will be accountable under the conditions laid down by law, the responsible ones will naturally seek the guidance both associations are prepared to offer.

Pilots need knowledge of Air Law to keep on the right side of the law, but also for the sake of flight safety.

The Other Side: PPL (A) Single Engine Piston (SEP)

And so we come to the end of our journey through the complexities of Air Law as far as the microlight pilot and aeroplane are concerned.

However, you may well meet up with pilots flying a different category of aircraft to that which you fly yourself and they may also hold one of those additional ratings referred to earlier.

In these circumstances the situation may arise when a statement you make on Air Law will be disputed by such pilots, so we will round off with a few sections of the law that can apply to them. On this occasion you can relax as you will be reading only from an interest point of view as the coloured panel on the following pages denotes.

Flight Conditions/Rules

Flight within the United Kingdom comes under two sets of defined flight weather conditions and flight rules according to the nature of the airspace in which the flight is being made.

The flight weather conditions are

Visual Meteorological Conditions (VMC).

When they fall *below* this minima they are known as

Instrument Meteorological Conditions (IMC).

The flight rules are

Visual Flight Rules (VFR)

Instrument Flight Rules (IFR)

At certain times operating within them can require that you have a Rating *additional* to your basic PPL.

Ratings

Instrument Meteorological Conditions (IMC) Rating

The IMC Rating allows a pilot to fly as PIC

- out of sight of the surface or in cloud

- on a Special VFR flight in visibility down to three kilometres – but not less

- on take-off and/or landing in visibility below cloud down to not less than 1500 metres.

Night Qualification

A Night Qualification entitles a pilot to be PIC of an aircraft flying at night. If passengers are to be carried, at least three take-offs and landings should have been made as PIC in the previous 90 days, at least one of which should have been at night.

Instrument Rating (IR)

The Instrument Rating entitles a pilot to be PIC of an aircraft flying in certain controlled airspace that requires compliance with IFR.

Visual Flight Rules (VFR)

Outside Controlled Airspace – within Class F and G airspace

Visual Flight Rules (VFR) state that an aircraft, other than a helicopter, may fly subject to the VMC minima laid out below.

Note: In the criteria that follows *each* stated limitation of visibility and horizontal/vertical separation from cloud requires compliance at the same time during any part of the flight.

a) Above Flight Level (FL) 100 there is no speed limitation, but the aircraft must remain

- with an in-flight visibility of at least eight kilometres

- at least 1500 metres horizontally from cloud

- at least 1000 feet vertically from cloud

b) At or below Flight Level (FL) 100 there is a speed limitation of 250 knots and the aircraft must remain

- with an in-flight visibility of at least five kilometres

- at least 1500 metres horizontally from cloud

- at least 1000 feet vertically from cloud

or alternatively

In the UK

In the UK, an aircraft may fly with a speed not exceeding 250 knots at or below 3000 feet AMSL, or 1000 feet above terrain, whichever is higher, but it must remain

- with an in-flight visibility of at least five kilometres

- clear of cloud

- in sight of the surface

however:

Within Class G airspace below 3000 feet, with a speed not exceeding 140 knots IAS, the limitations are as per the second alternative in (b) above except for the in-flight visibility limitation, which is reduced to 1500 metres.

Do remember that the alternatives within (b) apply within the UK only although it is possible that some other states may have adopted them. If you intend to fly abroad you should check to see if the country concerned operates under these or any other agreed alternatives.

To fly within the privileges of the Private Pilot's Licence (Aeroplanes) below the above VMC minima requires that you hold an IMC or Instrument Rating.

Inside Controlled Airspace
Within Class A Airspace
VFR not applicable

Within Class C, D and E Airspace – as follows:
An aircraft may still fly under VFR by day when it can conform with the following VMC minima:

- above FL100; have an in-flight visibility of at least eight kilometres

or

- below FL100; have an in-flight visibility of at least five kilometres

and in both cases

- be at least 1500 metres horizontally and 1000 feet vertically from cloud
- fly at a speed not exceeding 250 knots IAS below FL100
- have obtained ATC clearance in Class C and D airspace

Notes:

- Special VFR clearance may be obtained from ATC for flight in a Control Zone (CTR).
- An exemption exists in the UK only, which permits flight by aircraft in Class D airspace at or below 3000 feet AMSL at a speed of 140 knots or less, which remains clear of cloud and an in-flight visibility of at least five kilometres.
- Except when a Special VFR clearance is obtained, an aircraft may not take off or land at an aerodrome within a CTR (or enter the ATZ or circuit) if at the aerodrome, the cloud ceiling is less than 1,500 feet or the ground visibility is less than 5 km.

Instrument Flight Rules (IFR)/Altimeter Settings

For newcomers to flying, discussing IFR requires only a brief insight. Instrument Flight Rules apply when weather conditions become IMC unless a Special VFR is granted, or flight takes place in Class A controlled airspace, or the pilot elects to fly IFR.

Outside Controlled Airspace – within Class F and G airspace

a) Subject to low flying requirements the aircraft may not fly at less than 1000 feet above the highest obstacle within 5 nm.

Exceptions to the rule are

- taking off and landing
- when flying at or below 3000 feet AMSL,

clear of cloud and in sight of the surface

- when on a route authorised by ATC

b) At or below 3000 feet AMSL or below transition altitude, a pilot may use any altimeter setting, but beneath a TMA or CTA the QNH of an aerodrome beneath that area should be used.

c) Above 3000 feet AMSL, or transition altitude if it is higher, unless directed by ATC, a pilot will select a cruising level based on the altimeter set at the Standard Pressure Setting of 1013.2 mb and will express any vertical position report as a Flight Level (FL).

The flight level selected under the rules in (c) will be related to the aircraft's magnetic track in compliance with the semicircular level system. In this context, eastbound is considered to be less than 180°, whilst westbound is 180° and less than 360°. VFR and IFR aircraft are allocated different levels to fly at:

- IFR flights use whole 1000's of feet (e.g. 1,000, 3,000 etc. when flying eastbound and 2,000, 4,000 etc. when flying westbound).
- VFR flights use the intermediate 500 feet levels (e.g. 3,500, 5,500 etc. when flying eastbound and 4,500, 6,500 etc. when flying westbound).

For VFR flights, compliance with the cruising levels is recommended, but is not mandatory.

Inside Controlled Airspace – within Class A, C, D and E Airspace

a) The same as a) under 'Outside Controlled Airspace'

b) A flight plan must be lodged and ATC clearance obtained. The flight plan must be adhered to unless instructed otherwise by ATC.

c) Any switch from IFR to VFR can only be made if the flight can continue in uninterrupted VMC while in controlled airspace and ATC are informed that the flight plan is cancelled. This does not apply if the airspace is designated for IFR only (Class A).

d) Unless a flight plan is cancelled an aircraft commander must inform ATC on landing or leaving controlled airspace.

e) An aircraft flying under IFR, which is in, or intends to enter, controlled airspace must report time, position and flight level at such intervals and reporting points as directed by ATC.

Chapter 7
Human Performance Limitations

Introduction

The relatively slow speed and low operating altitudes of the normal microlight aeroplane may lead the student pilot to consider the subject of Human Performance Limitations (HPL) to be unnecessary. This is not so; we are all human and according to our state of health in general or at a particular moment there are factors which can affect our ability to fly safely and accurately. Certainly there are some aspects of the subject which can be immediately irrelevant but with the future in mind there can come a time when such knowledge is crucial. The student microlight pilot of today may well be the microlight pilot who attempts an altitude record at some time in the future and with the 'experience' gained by then there may be an apathy towards further study.

In this section every endeavour has been made to keep the subject relevant to the microlight aeroplane with its operating limitations in mind and the constraints under which it flies. Where the requirements of a medical may be touched upon they are worth noting even though they may not strictly speaking apply to the microlight pilot flying on a Declaration of Fitness.

First Aid

It is in the nature of airfields used by microlight pilots that assistance from the emergency services may be a significant distance and hence time away. All pilots should have a basic knowledge of the principles involved in providing first aid to those in need.

The agencies tasked with providing first aid advice constantly work at producing information that is both simple and effective. The detail of the guidance evolves with time, so it is essential to keep up to date by referring to current material.

As well as offering first aid training courses, the following organisations provide basic first aid information:

British Red Cross publishes an online resource called *Fast First Aid Tips* that is accessible via their website, www.redcross.org.uk.

St John Ambulance produces a free first aid guide that is available upon request via their website, www.sja.org.uk.

Human Requirement for Oxygen

That a human being must have oxygen to live is a statement of the obvious; but it is important when flying to understand where it may not be present in sufficient quantity to ensure you have adequate control of your actions.

The atmosphere to all intents and purposes is composed of 21% oxygen to 78% nitrogen; the other 1% being composed of carbon dioxide, water vapour, argon and so forth. In the chapter on meteorology the relationship of pressure, temperature and density is discussed and this has a bearing on the amount of oxygen your body can receive as you climb above the surface of the Earth.

To the fit person the effect of a lack of oxygen, known as *hypoxia*, will not normally make itself felt below 10,000 feet; however it can start to tell at 8000 feet if you are perhaps below par. At this lower height it is the ability to learn to take in something new that can be affected rather than the ability to practise previously acquired skills. Over 10,000 feet you must be aware of potential problems. The picture is thus:

Ground – 10,000 feet
An intake of normal air is sufficient except where, as previously stated, a learning process is involved.

10,000 – 33,700 feet
Oxygen must be added to the air inhaled.

33,700 – 40,000 feet
It is necessary to breath 100% oxygen.

Above 40,000 feet
100% oxygen must be taken in under pressure as air pressure is insufficient to force the gas into the body.

From your study of meteorology you will be aware that the higher you go, the more rarified becomes the air. The percentage of oxygen in the atmosphere remains the same but there is less of it. Also, the pressure is steadily reducing until there comes a time when it is insufficient to 'push' the gas into your lungs. It is then that it must be induced under pressure.

To keep the environment as near to sea level as possible, cabins of commercial and other high flying aeroplanes are pressurised. Thus an aircraft at 35,000 feet will have a cabin pressure equivalent to flying at below 10,000 feet.

Hypoxia
As the brain is the most susceptible part of the body to lack of oxygen it is one's judgement that will be first to suffer through hypoxia. At 20,000 feet the onset can be slow but at 30,000 feet the effects can be so quick as to be unnoticed. Symptoms can be the lips and fingertips turning blue.

The effects of hypoxia can be as follows.

- judgement becomes sloppy with a pilot unaware that performance is lacking. Also, decisions are made at a slower speed and

co-ordination of movements is less smooth as muscles become affected.

- the senses of touch, vision and hearing all begin to be affected.

- there can be a personality change where one's outlook ranges from a slap-happy approach to one of aggression.

- all the time consciousness is dropping away and death can result at high altitude if an oxygen supply is not restored in time.

This leads to discussing some of the ways in which the effects of hypoxia can be accelerated.

- smoking produces carbon monoxide which impedes the passage of oxygen to essential parts of the body. This factor is obviously avoidable by choice.

- the longer the time of exposure and the greater the altitude are naturally two ways which will speed up the effect.

- the energy demands of the body if greater than normal; for example crew members exercising themselves in physical activity about the aeroplane as opposed to those sitting down will be affected more quickly. Likewise a person who is unwell will be subject to greater energy demands in the combating of the illness. Again, cold makes greater energy demands on the body.

- the presence of alcohol in the body.

Hyperventilation
Over-breathing is technically known as *hyperventilation*. It is associated with exhaling or 'ventilating' more carbon dioxide than is necessary in the normal breathing process; it is not confined directly to a lack of oxygen as a basic cause. In fact, it can be argued that there can be occasions when the oxygen balance can be too high if too much carbon dioxide is expelled from the lungs. Hyperventilation can happen on the surface as well as at an altitude.

The effort to take in more oxygen can lead to over-breathing but hypoxia is not the only factor that can lead to this condition. It can be caused amongst other things by anxiety, air sickness, heat and vibration.

Taking anxiety in particular; it has just been named as a cause of hyperventilation but the situation can worsen as the anxiety of needing to breathe faster leads to further anxiety, resulting in a potential vicious circle. Signs of this problem are tingling at extremities of the body such as hands, feet, lips and there can be hot/cold feelings anywhere on the body. Pilot performance drops off and vision can become tunnelled or clouded.

Where confusion occurs in flight as to whether a pilot may be suffering from hypoxia or hyperventilation, the problem should be treated as hypoxia unless below 10,000 feet, where a determined effort must be made to regulate the over-breathing. In so doing normal breathing will be restored.

Barotrauma

As one ascends, the atmospheric pressure drops and as it does so any pocket of air trapped within the body will end up at a higher pressure than the air outside. If this air cannot escape to equalise with the outside air to restore equilibrium, then *barotrauma* is said to exist and it can create problems. This is particularly so where the ears and sinuses are concerned which can become blocked during colds or flu. Pilots with such ailments must not fly; doing so could eventually render them unfit to fly for many weeks.

A pilot should pay particular attention to the possibility of barotrauma in passengers during descent from altitude. Briefing them to swallow hard, or better still, hold the nose and blow hard with the mouth closed is to be highly recommended. If the ears do not clear it may be necessary to climb back up to reappraise the situation. Certainly the tips given should be started early in the descent and repeated at intervals; they should not be left until the last minute.

Within the body itself gases can build up through eating rich or spicy types of food and drinking beer. If the gases so produced cannot escape through the normal channels of mouth or rear then considerable pain and even fainting can result. If you are going to fly high – watch your diet.

Common Ailments

Following on from the ailments discussed under 'Barotrauma', apart from colds and flu, a pilot is unfit to fly when suffering from gastroenteritis, which may include the symptoms of diarrhoea, nausea, stomach cramps and vomiting. There is every reason not to fly when taking medication whether purchased by oneself or prescribed by the doctor. They will often have side effects which will impair the ability to fly safely. When in doubt, clearance from an aviation doctor should be sought.

Decompression

People who take up flying may be termed adventurous types and therefore likely to take part in other forms of exhilarating sports, for example scuba diving.

Breathing in this activity is by means of compressed air and without delving into the technicalities you should not fly within 12 hours of swimming by these means and you must wait 24 hours if you have been more than 30 feet under water.

Air Sickness

This form of sickness, also referred to as motion sickness, is said to stem from the motion one undergoes as opposed to the motion one is expecting. It is capable of being overcome by becoming adapted rather than by medication, which can hamper the flight performance of a pilot. If you do take medication then consult an aviation doctor as some forms of treatment are not suitable for the pilot of an aeroplane.

A form of sickness experienced in the air not related to the above may well be due to a first flight and the tension attached thereto; also a hot stuffy environment can be another cause. A pilot should pay particular care to passenger comfort and should terminate the flight if necessary rather than put a companion off flying for good.

Hearing

Noise is measured in a unit known as the decibel. We live in a noisy world and short-term exposure to loud noise can cause a temporary loss of hearing. Should exposure to a source of this nature be long-term then permanent deafness or loss of hearing can result. Such noise would be around 90 decibels and over.

The length of time that one is exposed to noise is not the only factor; there is the level to be considered as well. For example an increase of only 30% in a noise level of 90 decibels will do as much damage in 1 minute that the 90 decibels would do in 8 hours.

If you attend discos or indulge in listening to high volume stereo you are making a choice as to your exposure. If you work in a job or indulge in pastimes where there is a high element of noise attached, you would be well advised to consider ear plugs or defenders. Flying a microlight can be deemed to be in such a category. Use of radio need not be precluded by the addition of some form of protection for the ears.

Sight

A defect in sight does not pose a problem to a pilot as long as it can be corrected with spectacles or contact lenses. The medical requirement would expect a car number plate to be read at around 40 metres – a similar but stiffer requirement than the 23 metres required for driving a car.

Bifocals are the answer to those who need correction for both long- and short-sightedness. Care is necessary with this type of spectacles as some pilots have experienced difficulty during the landing phase when it is necessary to rapidly change from looking well ahead to a closer point of reference. Varifocals are another method of providing for the correction of vision over a range of distances. Some pilots have found that the grading of these lenses reduces peripheral vision and that greater movement of the head is required to ensure that an adequate lookout is maintained. If you are in any doubt you should contact an aviation medical examiner.

Care should be taken in the use of certain types of sunglasses which vary with the intensity of light. The delay in change from one format to another could cause a problem.

The use of sight in the air is covered in more detail later when the avoidance of aerial collisions is discussed.

Toxic Hazards

Although the microlight is basically a very open air form of flying with the engine more often than not placed to the rear of the pilot, there are some types which are quite sophisticated with cabins appearing on the scene and a tractor type format with the engine in front. The possibility of unwanted exhaust fumes must be considered – particularly when some ingenious form of 'cabin heating' may be considered as an offshoot from the exhaust system.

Carbon monoxide emitted from exhaust is colourless and has no smell but it can bring on headaches, breathlessness and eventually render one unconscious.

You may recall that hypoxia can be accelerated by smoking. The intake of over 20 cigarettes per day can create a situation where your reactions will be influenced by an induced oxygen-related environment which will be the equivalent of 3–4000 feet above your actual altitude. Again, this is an avoidable factor by choice.

Vapour from fuel and lubricants can make one drowsy when inhaled.

Blood Pressure

Treatment for blood pressure subsequent to regular monitoring need not preclude a pilot from flying after the necessary checks have been carried out.

Epilepsy

Although not strictly a disease, epilepsy is unfortunately associated, to a lesser or greater degree according to circumstances, with a distinct loss of consciousness. It is possible, however, that a pilot's licence would be granted provided such attacks are deemed to be sufficiently under control to permit driving a car.

Alcohol, Medication and Drugs of Addiction

There is a mistaken view that any amount of alcohol can be taken up to 8 hours prior to flying. This is far from being correct. The consumption of even the smallest amount of alcohol must not occur within 8 hours of flying, with proportionally longer if larger amounts are consumed.

The pilot who becomes alcoholic must seek treatment and can resume flying after it, although total abstinence would be essential from then on. Even when an alcohol dependency may not exist, the level of intake can still be damaging. Taking a 'unit' of alcohol to be half a pint of beer or a normal glass of wine, medical opinions consider that above the range 21 to 28 units for a man and 14 to 21 units for a woman per week can be damaging. When flying you should adhere to the lower figure.

It should be remembered that it takes the body at least 1 hour to dispose of 1 unit of alcohol. The maximum limit of alcohol permitted in a pilot's body is 20 milligrams of alcohol in 100 millilitres of blood, or 27 milligrams of alcohol in 100 millilitres of urine, or 9 micrograms of alcohol in 100 millilitres of breath – which is 25 per cent of the limit prescribed for driving a motor vehicle in the UK. To be completely sure of being below the limit for flying it would, therefore, be prudent for a pilot to abstain from alcohol for at least 24 hours before flying.

Concerning drugs, those which can have an effect on the brain, and are taken say for depression or neurosis, may preclude any flying as pilot/crew whilst being taken. A pilot wishing to resume flying would need to show a current record of good health and consult with an Aeromedical Examiner.

If intending to fly, seek authoritative medical advice when taking any form of drug; even a common cold treatment can contain antihistamines.

Drugs of addiction and so-called recreational drugs, which are illegal, cannot be entertained where flying is concerned due to the very nature of their effect.

Knowledge and the Senses

Just like driving a car, the pilot of an aeroplane makes decisions which result from assessing what is seen, heard, felt and even smelt followed by action in accordance with present knowledge previously gained. There are occasions when this sequence can incorporate several actions taking place at the same time. The degree to which this happens will depend on the depth of knowledge and the length of time such knowledge has been put into practice, namely experience.

When talking of 'experience' it is as well to understand that effective experience is based on accurate knowledge. In all walks of life one can meet people who will utter such words as 'I have 20 years experience'. This can be a dangerous state of mind. It can shut out an awareness that there is always something new to be learned, but in many cases where acquired knowledge has been faulty, it can be a case of possibly 1 year of experience followed by 19 years of perpetuating error!

Knowledge can be termed the fundamental requirement but faults in the senses can lead to a misuse of knowledge in the making of decisions. Consider the short-sighted pilot who may not spot a potential collision course or the pilot with a hearing problem which may lead to a failure or misinterpretation of an instruction given in the air or received from the ground.

Speed of perception and action can be affected by age. Forgetting experience for a moment, a pilot under 30 years of age will normally react more swiftly than one who is over 60.

Again, being ready for a decision-making situation leads to a much faster response. The microlight pilot who flies with a potential landing ground in mind in case of an engine failure will not be caught out should the power suddenly fail. Furthermore, the reactions will be smoother and safer as a result. The pilot who is not prepared for a situation will take longer to respond.

Attention to detail during flight can be less during an easy period, such as a leisurely cruise, compared with the attention that is sharpened up during a landing. Watch this point because the last thing one wants is a casual attitude when the potential of a mid-air collision is in the making during a more relaxed part of the flight.

One final point on sharpening up one's wits when the need arises. Airspeed on approach can be termed a critical factor but it will serve no useful purpose if all effort is geared up to watching the ASI; one may miss the aircraft that has just cut in ahead and below. There has to be an awareness of the need to look almost virtually in two places at once.

Knowledge and perception need to be good and they rely on a healthy mind and body. However, even these factors alone are not necessarily enough as they can easily be impaired by the bad cockpit environment or poorly laid out controls and instrument panel found in some aircraft; for example the rear seat of a flexwing microlight is a less easy pilot position than the front seat.

While the design of any cockpit should be ergonomically optimised, it is important that the function and correct activation of individual controls is unambiguous. The labelling, feel, colour and shape of individual controls are important to ensure their correct operation. Some aircraft even have flap controls that represent the aerodynamic surfaces that they actuate and undercarriage levers in the shape of the wheels they operate! The microlight pilot should be mindful that similar aircraft may have different cockpit layouts, so it is important to become familiar with a new aircraft and its cockpit layout before committing to flight.

Visual Perception

As we all know from our everyday experience things aren't always as they first appear! When evaluating the world around us we compare what we see for the first time to things that we have seen before. This tendency results in an attempt to make the picture fit our existing mental model of the world.

So, it's not actually our eyes that play tricks on us – it's our brain!

This effect is particularly striking when confronted with a runway that has unusual characteristics compared to our previous experience.

A runway that is particularly narrow will tend to appear longer than it really is. Conversely, a very wide runway will seem shorter than it is. These characteristics can also make judging the touchdown difficult. The wide runway will result in a belief that the aeroplane is lower than is the case, with the reverse occurring on a narrow runway.

A sloping runway can result in the pilot adjusting height on the approach to land so as to make the view ahead appear as it does when approaching a level runway. If the runway slopes up the tendency is to fly low in order to make the picture look normal. A down sloping runway may well result in an approach that is too high.

When flying to an airfield for the first time it is important to consult any information that is available. Always consider any unusual visual effects that may arise from the characteristics of the runway and the surrounding terrain. Preparation and anticipation are the keys to success.

A further example of being misled by our visual perception may occur when making an approach to land with an unknown tailwind. Our senses may be telling us that we are going too fast due to the higher than normal groundspeed. Accidents have happened simply because pilots have slowed the aircraft down in this situation – a disciplined pilot will constantly check airspeed on the approach,

To develop the theme further, our vision may be compromised in conditions of reduced visibility or light.

It is worth noting that one of the occasions when the eye fails to supply good information is when pilot looks into a hazy sky. Just like an autofocus camera, there is nothing for the apparatus to focus on. The eye muscles in this case tend to relax and the default focus is just a few feet ahead!

As illumination levels reduce, the cone photoreceptors responsible for our colour vision, and concentrated in the centre of the retina, become less effective. At the same time the rods, which are much more photosensitive and better at sensing motion, take over with their black and white vision. This can make it far more difficult for us to distinguish ground features in conditions of low light. The distribution of the rods on the outer edges of the retina also explains why it is our peripheral vision that is responsible for detecting movement.

By being aware of the limitations of our abilities to view the world around us and then process that information, we should be better placed to form the complete picture.

Disorientation

One does not have to be involved in flying for very long before hearing of the horrendous results that can come about by flying in cloud without the necessary instruments and training. The microlight pilot is forbidden to enter cloud but, without going into detail, should the temptation arise be sure that all control of the aircraft could be lost within a very short space of time.

Sight is no longer available to help the untrained pilot in an ill-equipped aeroplane and the other senses will quickly begin to mislead the 'intrepid' (?) aviator. Feelings will enter the picture, which will be totally divorced from what is actually happening and any reactions based on such feelings will accelerate a situation from which recovery may be unlikely.

Do not be tempted into cloud however innocent it may seem.

Avoiding the Airprox

At one time the near miss in the air was known as an 'airmiss'. This has now been changed to '**airprox**' – i.e. 'in the proximity of'.

The avoidance of potential collisions is drummed into a pilot from the outset. 'Look-out' is given a high priority in training and a pupil pilot who flies faultlessly but fails in this aspect will surely not pass a General Skills Test.

There is a potential for collision when two aeroplanes are close to each other in the air or even at a distance when certain factors are present.

Unless in a pre-arranged formation situation, the behaviour of a nearby aircraft that is unaware of your presence is unpredictable.

Should it be at the same altitude, a sudden change of heading on the part of the pilot who is ignorant of your presence has all the makings of a problem. So if for one reason or another you are going to be in close proximity to another aircraft, take steps to ensure your presence is known.

Avoidance of a collision where a distant aircraft can pose a threat requires not only an understanding of **what** is perceived but also **how** to perceive the situation in the first place – the latter being concerned with the behaviour of the human eye.

Whether an aircraft is flying straight and level, climbing or descending and at whatever speed and heading it may have adopted, there is a risk of a collision if one aircraft remains on a constant bearing in relation to the other.

You can identify this situation when you spot another aircraft which to all intents and purposes seems to be stationary in your vision with no movement across your cabin window or in relation to some other part of your machine if you happen to be sitting outside as is the case with most microlights.

The fact that it appears to be stationary makes it harder to notice in the first place. The only indication of a likely collision would be an awareness that it was growing larger in your vision but herein lies another problem. At the very high speeds at which the modern jet can travel the oncoming aircraft may not have grown large enough to be noticed until collision is unavoidable.

To give an instance of this speed problem, an aircraft flying at 600 kt towards another flying at 200 kt gives a closing speed of 800 kt. To the pilots maintaining 'look-out', each will appear as a mere dot within three seconds of an impact. There could be but a tenth of a second left when the aircraft is large enough to attract attention without its presence actually being sought after in a search.

A microlight may travel at a relatively slow speed of say 60 kt but a low flying military jet doing 500 kt still produces a closing speed of nearly 600 kt. For example, spotting a jet at 3 nm with a closing speed of 600 kt gives you less than 20 seconds before possible impact! A sighting at 5 nm and a closing speed of 500 kt still only gives you 30 to 40 seconds.

Should the jet be an aircraft such as a Tornado, then the wings could well be folded back and the image mass will be even less easy to spot. In the UK, where the recognised bands of height at which such a hazard can be met is advised as between surface and 500 ft AGL, the pilot has at least an opportunity to minimise the risk by keeping at 1000 ft AGL and above.

The resolution of this unpleasant prospect related to high speed aircraft lies in maintaining the best possible effective look-out and in so doing you may think you are viewing the whole sky at one time when continuously moving your eyes around. In fact when it comes to spotting such a minute dot as an oncoming aircraft, the **continuously** moving eye cannot cope.

To take in such detail the eye must be constantly moved to the various parts of the sky with a **pause** to take in the segment being searched at any given moment. Continuous movement of the eye will not achieve this aim.

If any part of the aircraft structure is in your line of vision this will call for head movement as well as eye movement. It takes very little to obscure the minute speck of a fast approaching jet.

Stress
The stress with which we are first concerned is not the arousal of excitement or heightening of tension at a critical point in a flight such as landing or an emergency being handled by an experienced pilot under normal conditions.

The stress we shall discuss is that which can affect judgement rather than enhance it – the stress synonymous with present day living and it affects individuals in different ways. It can come from within a person by virtue of their make-up or it can be imposed from outside. There is of course a close link between the two in the end result.

Taking that which can come from within, the pilot with a vivid imagination can undergo far more stress than the more phlegmatic one. The former may see and prepare for a host of problems which could arise but usually never do. Fear causes this form of stress and as fear stems from the unknown this situation can decline as the individual experiences problems and learns to cope. However, it is unlikely that such feelings will be eradicated totally because it is in the very 'nature of the beast' to feel that way.

The more phlegmatic pilot will not be so affected and consequently has a much less stressful flight. However, should an emergency occur the prepared pilot could be in a better position to cope due to the mental alertness already in place for a given situation – the more carefree one being left to think much more rapidly.

There is perhaps an element of truth in the saying that a pilot should always have a slight 'knot in the stomach' on take-off. It portrays an awareness and a respect for the air and the responsibility of taking an aircraft into that environment. One has only to consider the number of small boat rescue operations that take place off our coast when untrained 'sailors' take to the water blissfully ignorant of the potential perils of the sea.

Undue stress of the wrong sort will cause problems in flying because it can affect or influence judgement and decision making – even to the extent of inducing panic in an emergency.

Let us look at some of the outside influences that can lead to stress in recreational flying.

Competing
A pilot becomes caught up in trying to match others by flying in conditions within the capability of his companions but not within his/her own capability.

Deadline
Being caught out by time – the get-home-at-all-costs attitude despite deteriorating weather or the approach of nightfall. The number of pilots who have never made the deadline they saw as crucial is unfortunately very considerable.

Domestic

Problems in the family can cause considerable stress and the pilot who leaves home to fly an aircraft in a state of temper after a family row, concern over an illness or even worse a bereavement, will not be in a fit state to think clearly. It is imperative that the illusion is not nurtured that going aloft will relax one or take one away from such problems. The stress will be there and judgement will be impaired.

Low hours

The pilot who does not have the opportunity to fly frequently will be under much more stress than the one who is regularly in the air.

Fatigue

It surely must go without saying that fatigue through over-work, lack of sleep or poor diet will inevitably induce stress. The pilot can become subject to a failure to respond to events with the necessary speed and accuracy. The situation will further deteriorate if common ailments or poor health in general are present.

The amount of sleep needed varies considerably with each person. The older one gets the less sleep one requires we are told. But, the older one gets the less becomes the choice of times of sleep. A young shift worker may take varying sleep times in his/her stride but the older person cannot cope so well.

Where insomnia is involved, which can lead to fatigue, advice should be sought as any drugs prescribed must be approved and the nature of the cause of the problem identified. Just as drugs for common ailments can temporarily preclude flying, the same applies to drugs for inducing sleep.

Noise

Undue noise, and to this can be added vibration, will certainly be stress-inducing. Attention should be paid to the reduction of such problem sources.

Temperature

Excessive heat and excessive cold can cause discomfort and thereby lead to stress through an unsuitable environment.

Managing Stress

It is easier said than done for some but there are ways in which stress can be reduced and controlled. The dangers of doing so by the use of unprescribed drugs or the absence of medical advice has already been discussed.

Talking over one's fears and problems with a close friend or colleague can help enormously. Although it may come as a surprise to some, such conversation can reveal that others have the same concern but do not appear to show it. From such a revelation can come consolation in not being alone, but more importantly it can lead to learning how others have coped. Seeking professional counselling should not be ruled out.

Keeping fit provides a well-tuned healthy body which is much more able to cope with stress than one below par. Some pilots practise meditation and other such techniques. If a religious belief is present this may well help to control stress in the sense that the worries and concerns are looked at in a different context to the non-believer.

Experience and practice will definitely contribute to reducing stress – take the problem of the low-hours pilot mentioned earlier. It is well worth such a pilot swallowing pride and seeking regular check flights with an instructor. The most critical moment in flying is no doubt the landing. The pilot who builds up air time for the sake of keeping within the law is never going to have the confidence and thereby be as less stressed as the one who confines his limited flying to repeated practice of taking off and landing in the circuit.

Adrenaline Rush

When stress is induced by heightened arousal, perhaps by excitement, anxiety or even fear, this can cause an adrenaline rush. The release of adrenaline into the body increases heart rate (pulse) and breathing rate, making the senses more acute and preparing us for what is known as 'fight or flight'. While the principal effect is to prepare us to cope with the situation, the effect on the respiratory system can sometimes cause hyperventilation, covered on page 96.

Social Psychology

Social psychology deals with the inter-relationship of people and is primarily important when one considers flight deck personnel in a large aeroplane being able to work together harmoniously.

In a microlight such a situation does not exist but there is one aspect of psychology that does need to be considered: it is probably the most powerful urge in the human make-up, namely the ego. Participation in many adventure sports is simply undertaken to satisfy this urge and there is nothing wrong in that. Learning new skills and facing new challenges is healthy and can change the outlook of a humble office clerk into one that sees a managerial post achieved which might never have been the case.

It is when the ego-trip gets out of hand that problems can arise. A pilot is trained to fly and the aeroplane is designed to fly; but both are limited in what their performance can be if safe flight is to take place. Curbing the ego calls for self-discipline.

Unfortunately there is a mistaken impression that throwing an aeroplane about the sky, usually exceeding laid down performance limitations, is the criteria by which a 'good' pilot is judged. Never could such an impression be so wrong.

Aerobatic manoeuvres require special pilot training and they also require special aircraft in which to perform them. The pilot not in possession of both these requirements who feels the urge to emulate the 'masters' is not a good pilot. In so doing a lack of self control is displayed which means an inability to handle the aircraft intelligently.

Certainly in the case of prototype test pilots there is a need for stretching the aeroplane to its limits, but those who do so will be found to be the most careful and meticulously disciplined pilots on this planet with no desire to impress or be flamboyant.

With the over-confident pilot for whom flying has no fears there is the danger of being unaware of performance limitations – that is the ability to undertake certain actions. In such cases there is a need for a conscious self-discipline to be imposed on oneself. The cure can sometimes be accelerated by an unpleasant experience which provides a short sharp lesson. At the risk of appearing critical of over-confidence it must be acknowledged that in a war-time situation the element of recklessness can pay off; but in recreational flying there is no place for such an approach.

Another aspect of self-discipline was referred to earlier in respect of the low-hour pilot not being reticent about seeking a check flight or refresher training.

There will be times when two pilots fly together and it should be of no surprise that even experienced aviators make mistakes! It could be that a student is flying with an instructor, or a candidate is being assessed by an examiner, or an inexperienced pilot is just 'along for the ride' with a friend. Whatever the relative experience of the pilots, the message is always the same: speak up and listen out! No matter how inexperienced a pilot may be, they must tell the commander if they perceive a problem. Of course, the commander must be receptive to genuinely voiced concern. A second pair of eyes and ears is a valuable resource: even passengers should be briefed to assist with maintaining an effective look-out.

Regrettably, the result of a rebuttal of one's own Human Performance Limitations is often painful and irrevocable with the pilot becoming another statistic in the records.

For the very few who may not have heard the saying – take heed.

> **'There are old pilots and bold pilots,**
> **But – there are no old, bold pilots.'**

Chapter 8
Meteorology

Introduction

A jet airliner can plough through weather that a light aeroplane would find prohibitive. A light aeroplane or glider can take to the air when many microlights must remain on the ground. This makes meteorology (we shall call it 'met' from now on!) of great importance to the microlight pilot.

Met is an inexact science; this makes it a critical subject for any pilot to grasp throughout his/her flying life, not just the student period. In no way can you master all the variables of weather during an initial course, so it is not just a subject that you study for the sake of passing an exam.

Indeed, passing the exam should ensure that you have learned the basics; but from then on the crux of the matter is putting them into practice so that you can safely face nature and its foibles when taking to the air – particularly if you have a passenger on board.

A certain type of weather system may be forecast for your region which carries with it a basic type of weather; but local mountains or being near the coast and so forth are geographical features which can bring about variations in one type of system.

The subject has sometimes been dubbed by pilots as 'the one I have most trouble with'. The aim in this chapter is to get you to stick to the 'KISS' philosophy: Keep It Simple, Stupid!

We will start by looking at the atmosphere. The air through which you fly has weight, pressure, temperature and moisture. All these properties are constantly changing in value and they are factors which combine together to produce the most talked about topic on earth – the weather!

Air Density

Density is the weight of the molecules in a given mass (or parcel) of air. The name 'parcel' is used to describe a mass or volume of air simply because no one has yet thought of a better term! Density decreases as the air becomes thinner with height. Density is a factor that is not directly measurable by an instrument.

Density is also affected by temperature. When a parcel of air is heated it expands and the number of molecules in the original volume decreases (Figure 8.1).

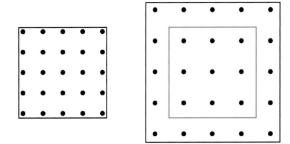

Figure 8.1 Expansion on heating

The reverse takes place when air is cooled.

Density is not to be confused with pressure. The latter is the weight of a column of air up through the atmosphere from the surface.

If at a given time the air in a column is heated the air will indeed expand but in so doing it increases the length (height) of the column. The weight in the column remains the same (Figure 8.2 on page 106).

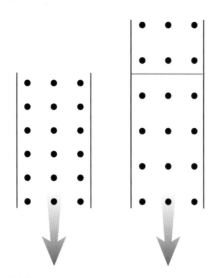

Figure 8.2 The column increases – pressure remains the same in both columns.

So we now see that density decreases

– with a decrease in pressure

– with an increase in temperature.

Finally, contrary to what you may imagine, the more water vapour present in the air the less dense that air will be, leading to a final conclusion that:

As relative humidity increases –
density decreases.

Pressure

The weight of air from the topmost limit of the atmosphere to the surface is termed **Pressure**.

The most common unit of measurement in the UK is the millibar (mb). However, the International Civil Aviation Organisation (ICAO) has changed to using the unit known as a hectoPascal (hPa), which is the same value as a millibar. As the UK has committed to utilising the hectoPascal, all further discussions of pressure will be referenced to hPa.

In the USA the measurement of pressure is measured in inches of mercury (inHg) which makes the ISA at mean sea level 'across the pond' read as 29.92 inHg. One hectoPascal approximately equates to 0.03 inHg.

Pressure Decrease with Height

In the lower levels of the atmosphere, pressure decreases by 1 hPa (0.03 inHg) for approximately every 30 ft (9 m) of ascent. After about 20 to 30,000 ft (6 to 9 km) the ascent would need to be 50–60 ft for a pressure drop of 1 hPa (0.03 inHg).

Pressure Measurement

Pressure readings are taken at regular intervals by day and night throughout the world at observation stations on land and at sea.

As pressure reduces with height, the altitude of each reporting station is taken into consideration so that each reading may be corrected to read as if it was at **Mean Sea Level (MSL)**.

In this way uniformity of readings is obtained from which a pressure pattern can be produced on a chart.

The instrument used to measure atmospheric pressure is called a barometer, of which there are three types.

Mercury

The mercury type of barometer is the most accurate as it is devoid of mechanical parts except for a vernier scale which assists in the reading of a measurement.

It consists of a column of mercury rising from a reservoir and kept in place by the atmospheric pressure. Readings are taken from a scale alongside the column.

Measurement of atmospheric pressure in inches has come from this form of barometer where the length of the column of mercury is measured in inches.

Aneroid

The aneroid barometer is limited in accuracy to a certain extent through the use of mechanical parts subject to friction. Basically it comprises a 'concertina' type of drum inside which air has been hermetically sealed at a fixed pressure. As the pressure inside the drum is constant the drum will contract or expand according to changes taking place in atmospheric pressure. The movements of the drum are transmitted by leverage and are shown visually on a dial (barometer) or through the trace of an inked pen on a chart placed on a rotating cylinder driven by clockwork (barograph). Both types have scales against which a reading may be taken.

Precision Aneroid

The modern observation station, previously equipped with a mercury barometer, will now have a precision aneroid.

This instrument is so sensitive it will react to being moved from the floor on to a shelf – perhaps no more than five feet higher.
It is sometimes referred to as a 'super-aneroid'.

Altimeter

At first sight you may think the altimeter is nothing to do with the weather; in fact it relies totally on atmospheric pressure to produce readings, and such pressure plays a major part in your flying future.

Unlike the barometer at a reporting station, which is static and has a permanent correction applied to it to obtain MSL pressure, the altimeter is very much a mobile entity. It will be subjected to a number of variables which must be understood if effective and safe use is to be made of it.

Some of the variables to be discussed are not strictly pertinent to microlights but they are worth noting if only to gain an awareness of what the 'other chap' has to face.

Atmospheric pressure at a given place is usually in a state of constant change. You will appreciate that the aneroid altimeter will respond to these changes and show corresponding changes in 'height' without ever moving. To cater for this situation, altimeters are fitted with a setting device which when set to the atmospheric pressure at the time will ensure that the altimeter is reading 0 ft on the ground.

For example:

- Pressure is reading 1000 hectoPascals and the altimeter is reading 0 ft.

- Pressure drops to 990 hectoPascals. This drop of 10 hPa at 30 ft per hectoPascal is equivalent to 300 ft.

- The altimeter will read 300 ft.

- Alter the setting scale to read 990 hPa and

the altimeter will once more read 0 ft.

For an aircraft that has been airborne for some time there is the likelihood that a pressure change has taken place since take-off. When radio is fitted this is no problem as a new altimeter setting can be obtained from the control tower.

The likelihood of a pressure change whilst airborne can have an effect on the flight path in relation to the ground.

For example:

- Pressure setting at take-off is 1000 hPa.

- Altimeter reads 0 ft.

- Course set for destination at 1500 ft.

- Pressure at destination is 990 hPa.

- Altimeter, if on ground, at destination would read 300 ft.

- An **actual** height of 1500 ft at destination would read 1800 ft on the altimeter.

- Pilot notices height 'increasing' *en route* and descends to keep at 1500 ft on the altimeter.

- Result – a **sloping** flight path towards destination.

- Actual height on arrival is 1500 ft less 300 ft due to pressure change = 1200 ft.

It needs no imagination to realise that any flight path that slopes downwards can pose serious problems to a pilot flying 'blind' on instruments. There may well be an obstruction *en route* which it is known will be avoided when flying at the planned height but would certainly be struck on an unplanned sloping flight path (Figure 8.3).

The example on the pressure change has presupposed the departure and destination airfields to be at the same height. You will appreciate that in practice this will rarely be the case.

In the last example had the destination been at 300 ft above the departure then the actual height on arrival would have been 900 ft.

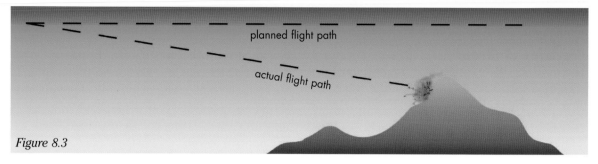

planned flight path

actual flight path

Figure 8.3

Altimeter Settings

It is obvious that safe flight for those having to rely on instruments demands constant contact with the ground to ensure up-to-date receipt of altimeter settings that not only cover atmospheric changes but also the difference that will be caused by different airfield levels.

There are four settings with which you should concern yourself. Although the fourth is mainly for IFR flights you need to know of it when in proximity to controlled airspace.

QFE

– Pressure at airfield level. Altimeter will indicate 0 ft when on the ground at the airfield.

– Used when in proximity of home or destination airfield.

– Reading from this setting is referred to as **Height**.

QNH

– Pressure corrected to MSL. Altimeter will indicate airfield elevation when on the ground at the airfield.

– Used mainly on routes below 3000 ft.

– Reading from this setting is referred to as **Altitude**.

Regional Pressure Setting (RPS)

– The UK is divided into a number of regions wherein a lowest QNH is forecast for a time period commencing at the start of the next hour and extending for a further hour. The RPS for each region is updated every hour. Such a region is known as an **Altimeter Setting Region (ASR)** and is marked on aviation charts.

Standard

– The standard setting is that laid down in the ISA definition and is used when flight takes place above the transition altitude in being at the time. When using this setting, the altimeter reading at a reporting point would be reported to ATC as a **Flight Level** based on 00's of ft. For example, 15,500 ft would be FL155.

– The standard setting is 1013.2 hPa – the altimeter scale would not cater for the defined Figure of 1013.25.

It is important that you should realise that the height of the 1013.2 hPa pressure level can vary enormously with pressure changes in the atmosphere. For example, FL45 may not necessarily be at 4500 feet above the ground; with an actual QNH of 993.2 hPa, the designated FL45 on your chart would be only 3900 ft **Above MSL (AMSL)**. So, approach this area at say 4000 ft on the QNH and you could soon end up where you should not be!

As a rough guide, when the QNH is less than 1013.2, the FL will be lower than its Figure depicts.

Absence of Pressure Setting Facility

In microlight flying, altimeters are sometimes used which have no pressure setting scale.

There are two basic criteria in cross-country flying which the lack of this facility may make it difficult to satisfy at first sight. They are:

– The need for flying on QNH for terrain clearance on route.

– The need for being on QFE overhead your destination in order to join circuit at the correct height.

The answer lies in compromise. Prior to take-off, adjust the altimeter to read the height of your departure point AMSL (QNH). As you proceed across country you will at least be flying as near to QNH as you can having made this adjustment.

On arrival over your destination or within the immediate vicinity of it **reduce** your altimeter reading by the height AMSL of that destination point as printed on your aeronautical map.

On touch down your altimeter should now read '0' which is what you require.

An example:

– Your departure point is 550 ft AMSL and your destination is 160 ft AMSL.

– *En route* there is high ground to be cleared at 800 ft so you plan to fly at 1800 ft to give the high ground a wide berth.

– Set your altimeter to read 550 ft (QNH). After take-off, a climb of 1250 ft will see you at your cruising altitude of 1800 ft.

– On arrival overhead your destination, reduce your altimeter reading by 160 ft (destination height AMSL) to read 1640 ft. Your altimeter will now be reading your height above the aerodrome (QFE).

Pressure Systems

From flying with eyes glued to the altimeter, now back to the ground! Earlier on we talked about how pressure readings were converted to Mean Sea Level readings to obtain uniformity in order to produce a meaningful pattern on a chart. This chart is built up by drawing lines which join places of equal MSL pressure at a

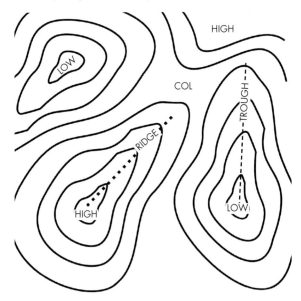

given time. These lines are known as **Isobars** and they resemble contour lines on a map.

A picture of a chart could emerge thus (Figure 8.4). A key to the chart labels follows.

High High pressure or anticyclone

Low Low pressure or depression

Ridge Wedge or tongue of high pressure extending out from anticyclone

Trough Similar to a ridge but extending from a depression

Col A neutral area between opposing systems.

Weather is very much associated with pressure systems so it is necessary to have a progression of charts for forecasting purposes.

Wind

Wind is nothing more than air moving from one place to another – a movement from an area of high pressure to an area of low pressure.

Take two tumblers – one full of water and the other empty. Join them with an imaginary tube at the base and both will end up holding equal amounts of water (Figure 8.5).

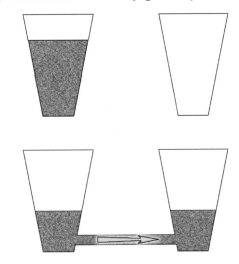

Figure 8.5

Air is a fluid and behaves as the water in the tumblers – flowing from high pressure to low pressure in order to establish equilibrium.

Other factors affect this simple analogy but they will be discussed later.

Let us examine the ways in which wind plays its part in microlight flying – for good or evil.

Wind Direction

The direction of wind is based on the point *from* which it is blowing (e.g. 240°). In terms of aviation this is expressed in degrees from 001° to 360° (Figure 8.6).

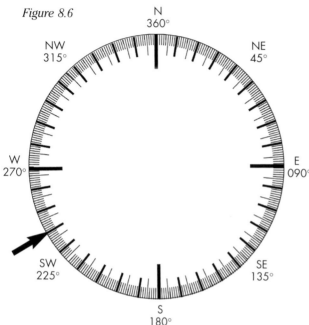

Figure 8.6

Changes in wind direction are known as **veering** when clockwise and **backing** when anti-clockwise. For example, when the wind direction changes from south-west to west it is said to have veered to the west.

Wind Flow

High and low pressure areas lie in approximate belts around the earth (Figure 8.7).

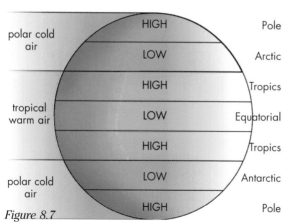

Figure 8.7

The rotation of the earth causes the flow to deflect and not move directly from high to low as you might expect. (Figure 8.8).

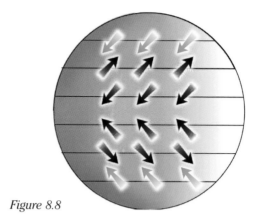

Figure 8.8

The rotational effect, combined with the effect of the air trying to move from high to low, results in a geostrophic effect which at 2000 ft and over causes the wind to flow around the isobars thus:

- Clockwise – around a high (Anticyclone)

- Anti-clockwise – around a low (Depression)

This flow is known as the geostrophic wind and is depicted in Figure 8.9.

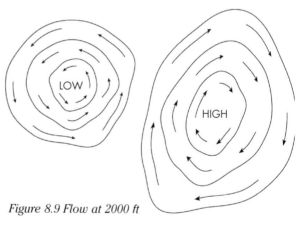

Figure 8.9 Flow at 2000 ft

Note: in the Southern Hemisphere these directions are reversed: clockwise round a low and anti-clockwise round a high.

The friction of the earth's surface reduces the geostrophic effect at ground level to the extent that over land the wind blows **in** towards a Low and **out** from a High at an angle of 30° to the isobars (Figure 8.10).

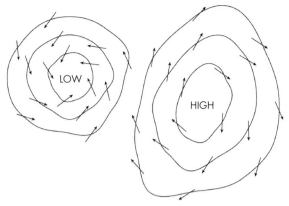

Figure 8.10 Flow at ground level

Over the sea the friction is less so the angle is only 10°.

For those who thirst after knowledge or are gluttons for punishment we will now take a closer look into why the air moves as it does from high to low pressure and why it is deflected.

The force governing this movement is known as the 'Pressure Gradient' (not to be confused with wind gradient) and it is steep when the isobars are close together; shallow when they are relatively far apart.

Whatever the gradient, if this were the only controlling factor, the air would instantly move from high to low with an almighty rush – only dying down as the low was filled.

Observation shows otherwise. Wind does not suddenly change in speed but only over a matter of hours – sometimes days. To all intents and purposes at any given time it can be said to be constant.

Now just as with an aeroplane flying at a constant speed where thrust is balanced by drag – so there is a force which balances gradient force in a wind flow.

This balancing force is known as Coriolis effect and is a result of the earth's rotation. It is not all that easy to describe but a brave attempt will be made to do so.

Imagine an object set in motion 'downhill' from the North Pole to the Equator but not in contact with the ground. Next, imagine this object being viewed from immediately below at point A on the Equator.

As the object moves down, the observer moves to A1, due to the earth's rotation. From A1, the object will appear to have descended and moved to the left in a clockwise direction. Continue this process in viewing the object from A2, A3 and A4 and note the direction in which the object appears to be to the observer passing through each of these points (Figure 8.11).

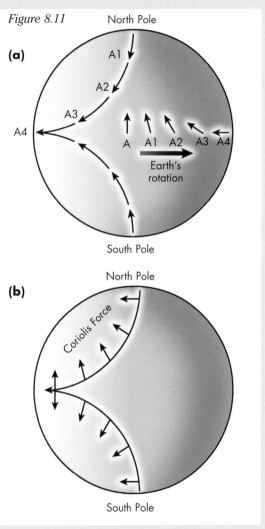

Figure 8.11

In (a) you can see the path of the object. Note how this path will be anti-clockwise if the object sets out from the South Pole.

In (b) you can see a force depicted which is acting perpendicular, or at right angles, to the object's path in order to pull it round into the curve.

This force is the Coriolis force or effect we have talked about and, you can see it is nil or neutral at the Equator.

Replace the object with a parcel of air which is on the move. As gradient and Coriolis forces must balance and as Coriolis effect is at right angles to the direction of any movement, you can see why wind blows along isobars and not across them (Figure 8.12).The above

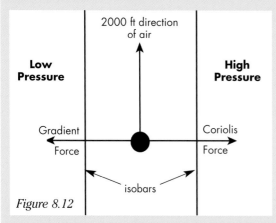

Figure 8.12

situation presupposes that the air is not in contact with the ground. If it were, such contact would result in a tendency to be caught up in the rotation thus reducing the Coriolis effect as far as exactly balancing gradient force is concerned. (Figure 8.13)

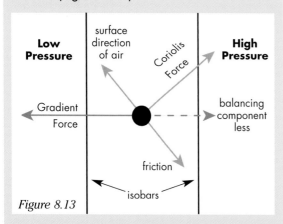

Figure 8.13

As Coriolis effect is always at right angles to any movement path you can see how the shift in Coriolis causes a change in wind direction at the earth's surface. Friction now plays a part in the balancing force needed to maintain a constant wind speed, as you have just seen.

On an Ordnance Survey map where the contours are close together they are depicting a steep rise or fall of ground. So it is with isobars on the chart – the closer they are together the steeper the rise or fall in pressure over a given distance and in consequence the stronger are the winds.

A rough guide to a centre of low pressure's position is to stand with your back to the wind – the centre will be to your left.

The rule is very useful in another way. You are flying with a strong wind on your port side. This is indicative of flying towards a low pressure centre which in turn means that your altimeter will begin to read high. If you are not aware of what is happening, you could adjust your altitude to maintain a constant reading and in conditions of poor visibility in the vicinity of high ground this would be very dangerous as you would be descending.

Apart from winds caused by pressure systems over a large area there are also more localised winds, often appearing contrary in direction to the prevailing wind at the time.

Katabatic Wind
– Colder air from the tops of mountains, being more dense rolls down the slopes into the lower ground of valleys. This phenomenon is more frequent at night.

Anabatic Wind
– Air in valleys warms up more quickly than air on the mountain tops. This less dense air then moves up the valleys and slopes rather as air moves upward due to uneven heating. An anabatic wind is sometimes referred to as a Valley Breeze.

Windspeed
Wind speed in aviation terms is expressed in nautical miles per hour – knots. When requesting official wind information you will receive it in degrees/knots; for example 240/15.

Airspeed
It so happens that many microlights still have airspeed indicators (ASIs) calibrated in statute miles per hour (mph). By law every ASI in the cockpit has to have a card clearly stating the calibration of the instrument.

If your aircraft manual happens to show the performance figures in knots (kt) and you find yourself facing an ASI in mph then you have a little mental arithmetic to do.

As knots will obviously be the 'in-thing' for the future we will confine any speeds in this book to using this unit. This will be particularly necessary when covering Navigation where nautical miles are the norm. A nautical mile is equal to 1.143 statute miles; but to help out here is an approximate conversion table (8.1).

Effect of Wind

We will now look at the effects that wind can have upon you in flight.

Windspeed v. Airspeed

Until airspeed reaches flying speed your aircraft will remain firmly on the ground. Obviously the quicker you can reach flying speed, the less will be the space required to do so. This is where wind comes in.

By pointing the aircraft **into** wind for take-off there will already be an airspeed passing over the wing to produce lift without any ground speed being generated at all.

Table 8.1

mph	knots
10	9
15	13
20	18
25	22
30	26
35	30
45	39
50	44
55	48
60	54
65	57
70	61

This is best demonstrated diagrammatically where our aircraft reaches flying speed at 45 kt (Figure 8.14 a, b, c below).

a) Aircraft is airborne in about three-quarters of space available.

b) Wind contributes to airspeed and aircraft is airborne in about half the space available.

c) A take-off downwind means starting off with a minus airspeed. In this situation the

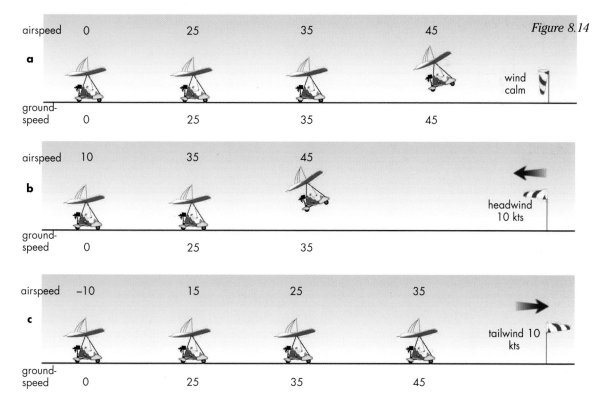

Figure 8.14

aircraft can run out of space before enough airspeed can be attained to sustain flight. Downwind take-offs require sufficient space to build up the faster run needed and should be thought out very carefully before being attempted.

The same situations apply to landings. Into-wind landing runs mean touching down at slower ground speeds and therefore result in shorter runs for pulling up. They allow you to land in a much smaller space.

Crosswind

A crosswind is said to exist when the wind is not directly in front of or behind the aircraft.

At take-off the aircraft's wheels are on the ground until flying speed is reached. As the crosswind meets the 'into-wind' wing the presence of dihedral will cause that wing to lift allowing a rolling movement to develop. This roll can be accelerated by the wheel acting as a pivot (Figure 8.15a).

The result will vary according to the type of aircraft. It will either weathercock into wind or turn and attempt to go with the wind. One way or the other there will be extreme difficulty in keeping to the original flight path. Added to this will be the likelihood of a wingtip touching the ground in the process (Figure 8.15b).

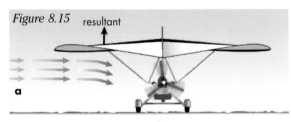

Figure 8.15   resultant

a

roll

b

If flying speed has been reached the aircraft will have become airborne and unless the movement is immediately countered it will drift downwind (Figure 8.16).

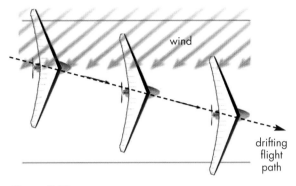

wind

drifting flight path

Figure 8.16

Should the wind speed momentarily drop there will be a corresponding momentary drop in airspeed and the aircraft could sink back onto the ground. In this situation the wheels will be out of line with the flight path and will strike the ground at an angle instead of head on.

The result is rather similar to that depicted in Figure 8.15 except the roll will be accelerated by the wheel striking the ground at an angle (Figure 8.17).

Crosswind landings and take-offs are not impossible but they do require some added skill and their success will be very much governed by the crosswind characteristics of the particular aircraft.

For example, an aircraft fitted with ailerons or spoilerons is able to lower a wing into the wind causing the wing to slip into that wind and to a large extent negate the crosswind effect.

There is no doubt that this form of control permits flying in conditions that would ground some microlights.

Wind Shear

Wind shear refers to a change in both direction and/or speed of wind, being called **vertical wind shear** when related to changes with height and **horizontal wind shear** when changes take place at the same level.

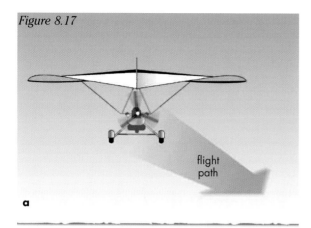

Figure 8.17

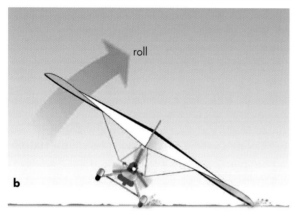

a

flight
path

roll

b

However, for many years the name given to vertical wind shear when close to the surface has been **wind gradient**, and it is quite likely that when talking to pilots from not so far back you will continue to hear this term being used. Perhaps it is now the time to catch up with modernity and fall into line with the official terminology. (Personally, being from 'way back', I find this to be difficult!)

Vertical Wind Shear

The simplest way to explain vertical wind shear close to the surface is to ask you to take a pack of playing cards and with a swinging movement drop it over a card table. The result will be self evident. The bottom card of the pack will virtually stop dead as it touches the cloth surface of the card table and each card up the pack will travel that much further than the one underneath it, with the top card travelling the most distance.

Wind behaves in the same way. Friction caused by the ground slows the wind speed at the surface with an increase taking place the

higher one goes.

The true speed is reached somewhere around 2000 feet. The maximum drop in speed occurs very close to the surface and must be considered very carefully on every take-off and more so on every landing.

Here is another analogy based on water. A boat 'underway' at a steady speed of say 10 knots through the water suddenly meets a current of 4 knots head on. For a brief moment, due to the initial impetus of the boat, the speed through the water will be 14 knots until the effect of meeting the current has worn off and the boat reverts to a speed of 10 knots once again.

So it is with an aircraft taking off and landing. On take-off it will climb into the faster moving air and show a temporary increase in airspeed. You may be tempted to reduce airspeed only to find yourself at a lower airspeed than you originally had because at that moment the effect of gradient wore off.

On landing, the effect can be more critical. You are descending on the approach prior to touch-down and you lower into the level of reduced windspeed near the ground. You will feel the aircraft beginning to sink very rapidly and may be tempted to raise the nose to stop the sink; but what is happening is this. Temporarily your airspeed has dropped and should you be close to your stalling speed at the time a stall may well result, particularly if you raise the nose and so increase the angle of attack. This is the last thing you want at low altitude (Figure 8.18).

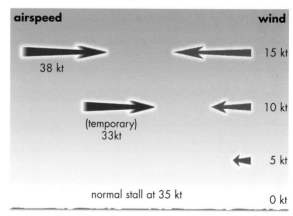

airspeed   wind

38 kt   15 kt

(temporary)
33kt   10 kt

        5 kt

normal stall at 35 kt   0 kt

Figure 8.18

Another situation where vertical wind shear can have an adverse effect is when close to the ground. In a banking turn the upper wing will be travelling faster and will also be in an area of higher windspeed than the lower wing. If the speed of the lower wing falls below stalling speed whilst the upper wing continues to produce lift, the result will be obvious.

Even if your airspeed is well above stalling speed the different lift forces on the respective wings can cause overbank which aileron input cannot overcome at the time. The lesson is no banking below say 150 feet.

Horizontal Wind Shear

Conditions in the atmosphere can exist which give rise to sudden changes of wind direction at the same height – including ground level.

At great heights the effect is largely navigational but at low level it can prove critical even to the largest jet airliner set up on its final landing run.

On a conventional approach into wind you have just seen how vertical wind shear can cause a fall in airspeed. The same effect can be brought about by a change in wind direction, as any such change will bring about a reduction in the value of the head wind component (Figure 8.19).

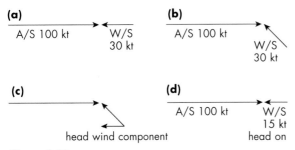

Figure 8.19

Taking (a) we have the normal pattern of events.

In (b) a horizontal wind shear has taken place.

At (c) you will note that the effect is now part cross and part head-on as far as the aircraft is concerned.

In (d) can be seen the value of the head wind component and to all intents and purposes there has been a drop in windspeed of 15 kt.

The effect on the aircraft will be the same as that of vertical wind shear in terms of loss in airspeed, but as horizontal shear is less predictable it is consequently more hazardous.

Normally in the landing configuration wind shear is caused by severe local thunderstorms, which can have a marked effect on wind direction in a very localised area. Sufficient to say that a microlight should not be airborne in such weather.

Low Level Turbulence

The atmosphere is rarely at rest particularly near to the ground. You have only to watch the smoke from a chimney stack to have proof of this fact.

The surface of a deep river looks placid yet it can be hiding considerable turbulence taking place on the bed. If the river is shallow the behaviour of the water close to the bed is more readily apparent. Ripples, waves and eddies caused by rocks and ruts are all visible to the eye (Figure 8.20).

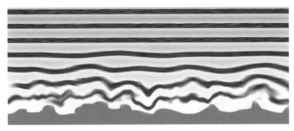

Figure 8.20

Picture the atmosphere as being this river and the 'bed' or surface the rocks and ruts are hedges, trees and buildings. Air behaving as a fluid will form the same ripples and eddies as the water and these can cause trouble for microlights (Figure 8.21).

Figure 8.21

You should always have a mental picture of what the air can be doing when you are flying low near obstructions. Low level turbulence can be caused by another factor. Look at a fire burning out of doors. You will see air shimmering above it with particles of ash shooting upwards. This is because air heated to a greater degree than its surroundings, becomes less dense than the surrounding air and rises.

Uneven surface heating does not necessarily need fire to trigger off turbulence. An example of a natural source is simple; on a sizzling hot summer day would you rather sit on a rock outcrop or on the grass? No prizes for the answer. The air around the rock is going to become much warmer than the air around the grass and consequently it will rise.

Obviously, with some of the air remaining static and some on the move vertically, you have a turbulent situation in the making without wind or obstructions playing a part.

On an airfield, runways, grass and buildings can all be sources of uneven heating.

You will have gathered that virtually all that has been said so far has been related mainly to wind. Indeed, in the early stages this is really something you need to know from the outset. To cater for the sceptics perhaps Table 8.2 will highlight the problem.

Table 8.2

Type of Aircraft	Cruise Speed	Wind Speed	Effect
Jet airliner	500 kt	20 kt	4.00%
Light aircraft	100 kt	20 kt	20.00%
Microlight	50 kt	20 kt	40.00%

Remember that in all the effects of wind that have been discussed the stronger the wind – the greater the effect.

Hill Lift/Leeward Side of Hill

Wind has so far been talked about as being more of an enemy than a friend. However, you are now considered to be much more experienced and ready to make use of the opportunities that wind can sometimes offer.

Ask any glider or hang glider pilot what they think about hill lift and they will normally go into raptures as it is a prime way in which they can remain airborne for virtually as long as they like.

Many microlights are akin to gliders and hang gliders in that in spite of the added weight of an engine they still have a very reasonable sink rate when the power is off.

Hill lift is a component acting as a result of wind being forced up a slope (Figure 8.22).

In (a) you are looking at the obvious – wind moving up and over a hill lying in its path.

In (b) you are looking at a breakdown of the forces involved.

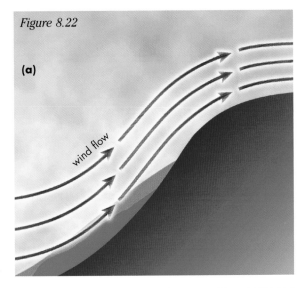

Figure 8.22

(a)

wind flow

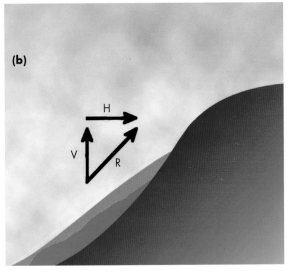

(b)

H

V

R

R – the resultant caused by the hill.

H – a horizontal component of that resultant.

V – a vertical component of that resultant and the most important one as far as we are concerned.

For example, wind travelling at around 30 ft per second (20 mph) up a 45° slope could produce a vertical component of some 20 feet per second (fps) in a given area above the slope.

Gliding down at 10 fps through the air which is rising at 20 fps would result in your aircraft ascending in relation to the ground at a rate of 10 fps as long as it remained in that rising air.

The area of best hill lift is usually to be found about one-third out from the top of the hill in relation to the foot of the hill.

It does not take much imagination to realise the opportunities that hill lift offers the microlight pilot. With the engine throttled right back a considerable amount of air time can be enjoyed with the minimum amount of fuel being used.

There have been occasions when light aircraft pilots with soaring experience have made use of hill lift in times of engine trouble. They have been able to stretch their flights, giving more time to select a suitable forced landing site and in some cases they have actually been able to reach their destination where it has been in the vicinity of the hill range.

What goes up must come down – there is always the other side of the hill. Just as air will climb as it meets the windward slope so it will descend down the leeward side. This time the vertical component will be acting in the opposite direction – it will not be lift, it will be a downdraft.

You must be ever conscious of your position in relation to hills. On the leeward side you may be cruising at the correct airspeed only to find yourself descending at an unhealthy rate in relation to the ground.

An instinctive reaction at that moment may be to climb which could lead to a stall – the downdraft may be too powerful for your aircraft's engine to pull you up. There is only one

course of action you must take – act contrary to instinct, increase your airspeed and head downwind away from the slope to escape the effect (Figure 8.23).

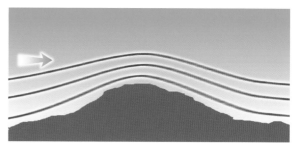

Figure 8.23

Wave Effect

Turn your thoughts to the river once again. When ripples are created by an obstruction they can carry on downstream reaching quite long distances from the cause.

So it is with the air. Given certain atmospheric conditions the air will travel in a wave motion for some considerable way downwind from the hills that set the motion in being (Figure 8.24).

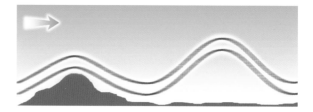

Figure 8.24

Standing waves as they are called can reach considerable heights and are much used by sailplane pilots wanting to cover long distances. Each wave will produce lift on its windward side and a downdraft on the leeward side.

The uninitiated power pilot is often bewildered to find his rate of ascent or descent quite dramatically changing although the cruising speed and engine revs are constant and there are no hills in the immediate vicinity. If a quick look at the map indicates hills some distance upwind then a wave should be presumed and the flight path adjusted up or downwind to a point out of the wave effect.

If this effect is experienced in closer proximity to the hills then the move should be downwind only – to avoid any rotor problems that could arise in the immediate lee of those hills.

Rotor Effect

A far worse situation can be encountered should the lee side be in the form of a relatively sudden drop. Remember the river bed where in the immediate vicinity of rocks and ruts there were eddies set up – not smooth ripples.

The smooth flow will break up and the air will behave quite wildly, creating a rotor effect in which you may not only be forced down but also lose control in the rough air (Figure 8.25).

Figure 8.25

Wake Turbulence

A final factor, which is not specifically caused by wind but is certainly associated with it in terms of avoidance, is **Wake Turbulence**.

This by definition is the disturbed air left behind any aircraft caused primarily by vortices generated at each wing tip, and also by propeller slipstream or jet exhaust. It has the power to cause total loss of control and must never be under-rated.

This area of turbulence rotates along its track, widening as it does so (Figure 8.26).

Figure 8.26

It will track with the wind (Figure 8.27).

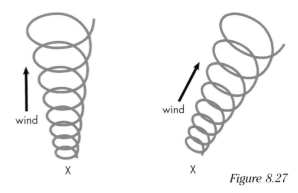

Figure 8.27

Normally vortices descend gradually and can exist 2 to 3 miles behind the aircraft that is the creator of the effect. They will be particularly strong with microlight aircraft. They will be affected by atmospheric conditions, the nature of which from a terminology point of view is explained later (Figure 8.28).

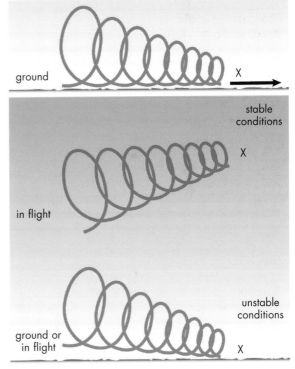

Figure 8.28

If you are left with no alternative but to land behind another aircraft taking off, then make every effort to touch down at the very beginning of the runway. This creates the largest possible gap between you and the other machine in which atmospheric conditions may have had a chance to dissipate or at least reduce the effect.

Your best method of handling wake turbulence is to avoid it at all costs by never taking off or landing immediately following another aircraft.

Bear in mind that this condition exists in flight as well as on the ground so conjure up a mental picture of its likely track. Select a path upwind of the preceding aircraft and/or below its track, according to the atmospheric conditions.

The helicopter is a particularly dangerous source of turbulence at all times.

The official figures laid down for separation in time and distance for wake turbulence are as follows.

Take-Off:
– From same spot as preceding aeroplane, allow 2 minutes.

– From any intermediate part of the runway between the preceding aeroplane's start point on that runway and its lift off, allow 3 minutes.

No separation distances are involved at take-off.

Table 8.3 Landing Approach: based on the type of aeroplane you are following

Aircraft	kg	Separation
Heavy	>136,000	7 nm
Medium	>40,000	6 nm
Small	>17,000	4 nm

No official figures exist as yet for microlights but suffice to say if larger aircraft require these times and distances then the microlight pilot must certainly consider increasing them on those occasions when the risk is possible.

Remember, vortices come from induced drag and thrive on a low aspect ratio wing with a high angle of attack at low speed – all the ingredients for warning you that one microlight has to be very careful in following another.

Temperature

Contrary to popular belief the atmosphere is not heated directly by the sun. The sun heats the earth and the earth heats the atmosphere on the principle of a radiator.

This fact is made more apparent when one realises that the higher one goes the colder it becomes – in other words, one is colder on moving away from the 'radiator'.

The seasons play a part in the amount of heat put into the radiator. In summer, in the British Isles, the sun is high in the sky and the days are long. In winter, the sun is at a low angle and the days are short. Naturally, the longer the sunshine each day, the hotter becomes the 'radiator' (Figure 8.29 page 119).

Cloud acts as an insulator – it can reduce the amount of heat taken in and it can also reduce the amount that radiates or escapes into the atmosphere at night.

Measurement
Temperature in the UK is reported in **Celsius** expressed in degrees (°C). In the USA the Fahrenheit (°F) standard is still in use.

The ISA temperature is defined as 15°C (59°F) at Mean Sea Level (MSL).

Lapse Rate
Lapse Rate (LR) is the name given to the rate at which temperature drops with height. It is constantly changing according to the nature of the air mass existing at the time.

It is important in forecasting so regular readings above given locations are taken several times a day by aircraft or balloons equipped with radio.

Inversion
Inversion is a situation where temperature is seen to increase with height. This is usually the result of warm air, which is less dense, climbing over colder air. It can also come about nearer the ground when the ground cools rapidly in the evening through radiation and the air immediately in contact with the ground is colder than that above. Inversions are particularly noted for trapping fog and haze and causing bad visibility. They are normally associated with anticyclones.

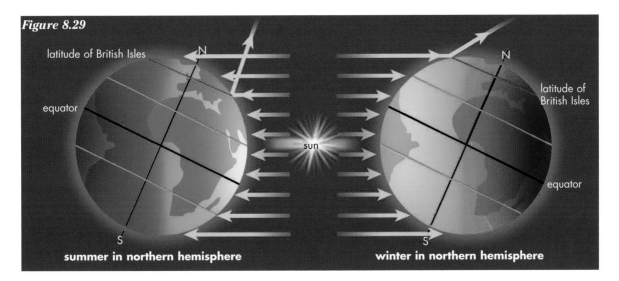

Figure 8.29

latitude of British Isles

equator

sun

S

summer in northern hemisphere

N

latitude of British Isles

equator

S

winter in northern hemisphere

The Troposphere

Cloud formation and weather only occur within a limited belt of the atmosphere.

This belt is known as the **Troposphere** and is distinguished from the rest of the atmosphere by the fact that within it there is a definite temperature lapse rate which by the ISA standard is accepted as 2°C per 1000 ft (1.98°C to be exact) up to the **Tropopause**.

The tropopause is the transition line, not a belt, between the Troposphere and the Stratosphere.

Above the tropopause lies the **Stratosphere** where, in its lower layers up to around 69,000 ft (21 km), the temperature can be relatively constant.

Referring back to the tropopause, its height above the Earth's surface, and therefore the depth of the troposphere, in the temperate latitudes is around 36,000 ft (11 km). This figure varies considerably with the regions being only about 30,000 ft (9 km) at the Poles but

over 52,000 ft at the Equator.

Similarly, the tropopause is affected by the seasons – being higher in summer and lower in winter.

It is also higher above the warm sector of a frontal system.

These variations are shown in Figure 8.30.

From a flying point of view the variations in the tropopause may seem academic. However, you have only to experience a tropical thunderstorm to realise how convection being able to reach higher levels can produce much more violent weather. To a lesser extent you can witness a quite effective example in the British Isles by noting the height to which cumulo-nimbus reach up in summer compared with winter.

Adiabatic Lapse Rate

When an amount or 'parcel' of air is *forced* to ascend or descend it will be affected by a decrease or increase in pressure. Before we go any further, consider the following analogies.

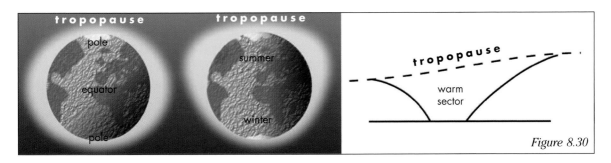

tropopause   tropopause

pole

equator

pole

summer

winter

tropopause

warm sector

Figure 8.30

When using a bicycle pump you will soon be aware of how hot it becomes without any extra heat being introduced around it. Without delving into the realms of physics, you can appreciate the fact that as pressure is increased inside the pump – so is the temperature.

The reverse happens when a decrease in pressure takes place – there is a loss of temperature even if there is no external loss of heat introduced to the surround. The way a refrigerator can work demonstrates this where the removal of air reduces pressure and thus creates the required chill.

Having established these facts we can proceed.

So when a 'parcel' of air within the atmosphere is forced to ascend through having to cross over hills or by uneven heating as discussed earlier, the pressure will decrease and the temperature will do likewise. This form of cooling, with no outside factor involved except the decrease in pressure, is known as **Adiabatic Cooling**. This cooling takes place at *fixed* rates for dry and wet air.

The difference between dry and wet air for our purposes is as follows:

– Dry air is air which may contain moisture but has not yet reached the point where the moisture content condenses into cloud.

– Wet air is air whose moisture content has condensed into cloud.

Having established the distinction it is possible to give figures for the two adiabatic lapse rates.

– **Dry Adiabatic Lapse Rate (DALR)** is a constant 3°C (5.4°F) per 1000 ft.

– **Saturated (Wet) Adiabatic Lapse Rate (SALR)** is a constant 1.5°C (2.7°F) per 1000 ft until at about 6000 ft where it begins to increase. Finally at around 30,000 feet it will be the same as the DALR.

Why the difference, you may ask? The best analogy to describe this occurrence is to ask you to recall what happens when you have washed your hair and you then apply an electric dryer to it. Alternatively, recall how you feel on coming out of the sea on a hot summer day as you lie on the beach to dry.

In both cases you will feel a distinct coolness until you are dry. The reason is that evaporation, which is what is happening, uses up heat – hence the cooling effect. To explain the difference in the two adiabatic lapse rates we must look at the opposite to evaporation, namely condensation.

When condensation takes place, heat is given off known as latent heat. This latent heat is sufficient to reduce the rate of cooling in air where condensation is taking place by about half. Hence to 1.5°C (2.7°F) in saturated conditions compared with 3°C (5.4°F) dry – until around 6000 ft.

The different types of lapse rates are important in understanding the formation of cloud so no excuses are offered for elaborating on the subject.

Incidentally, before moving on, do bear in mind that similar changes take place within descending air where the process would now be termed **Adiabatic Warming**.

Temperature Winds
Sea Breeze Effect
The air over the land heats more quickly than the air over the sea. The warm air rises and the cooler air from the sea flows in to replace it. The effect does not normally penetrate far inland but there are exceptions.

Uneven Wind
This is similar to sea breeze effect but can occur anywhere. Uneven heating causes air to rise and cooler air flows in from all round to fill the gap. The sudden lifting of a windsock on a calm summer day is often an indication of a convection wind. It is shortly followed by a return to calm as a balance is restored. More on this later.

Relative Humidity
This was touched on slightly in discussing lapse rates. Relative humidity is the amount of water vapour present in a given mass of air expressed as a percentage of the total amount of water vapour that mass could hold before becoming saturated.

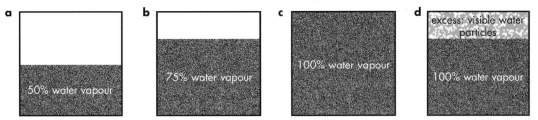

Figure 8.31

Temperature has a great bearing on the amount of water vapour the air can hold (Figure 8.31).

Take a mass of air at a given temperature and assume that this air contains 50% of the total water vapour it can hold. It is thus said to have a relative humidity of 50% (Figure 8.31a)

When cooled, air can contain less water vapour. Hence, the same water vapour content *increases* relative to the maximum amount of such vapour in the air can hold (Figure 8.31b)

On yet further cooling the water vapour content can eventually reach the point where the air is only just able to contain it. The air is now said to be saturated with a relative humidity of 100% (Figure 8.31c)

The temperature at which the air becomes saturated is known as the **dew point** temperature.

Still further cooling will produce more water vapour than the air can hold. At this point **condensation** can take place where the excess invisible water vapour converts into visible water particles as cloud. If at ground level, it will be fog or dew (Figure 8.31d)

For any condensation to take place there must be minute particles of matter (e.g. dust) present in the atmosphere – known as **condensation nuclei**.

Effect of Density on Flight

Having now covered pressure, temperature and humidity which all have an effect on density, it is time to look at the latter's effect on flight.

So what effect has density on flight? If it decreases, the air passing over the wing becomes thinner and likewise the number of air molecules entering the air speed indicator (ASI) will be less than normal. The ASI reading will now reduce to below your actual speed through the air which is True Airspeed. (See page 64.)

During take-off, to bring the indicated airspeed up to flying speed, for sufficient lift to permit take-off, means increasing the groundspeed. In so doing the take-off distance will now increase and there will also be a reduction in climb rate in the thinner air compared with that shown in the aircraft manual.

Performance figures shown in such manuals assume the use of a *hard* runway and are all based on the International Standard Atmosphere figures which you should use as a yardstick. When the airfield pressure is **less** than 1013.25 hPa and/or the temperature is **greater** than 15°C (59°F) the air density will have **decreased**. Here is an example of the effect.

Take a *grass* airfield 500 ft AMSL with an air temperature of 25°C (77°F). The decrease in density due to the height of the airfield AMSL and the increased temperature above 15°C (59°F) would increase the take-off run in still air by 60% and decrease the rate of climb by 25%.

To sum up, you have a high altitude airfield on a hot sticky day with the friction of wet grass instead of a smooth hard runway. These factors should make you think deeply as to whether you can get airborne from your strip and then clear any obstacles ahead on climb-out.

Clouds

When talking about clouds we are entering into the more visible aspects of meteorology.

With wind or temperature we can feel and experience their effect, but cloud we can actually see and, with experience, be able to interpret the signs each type provides.

Clouds are classified by the height of their base. The three classifications and their base heights are officially defined as in Table 8.4.

Table 8.4

Low cloud	Surface	to 6500 ft (2 km)
Medium cloud	6500 ft (2 km)	to 23,000 ft (7 km)
High cloud	16,000 ft (5 km)	to 45,000 ft (14 km)

The wide range of base heights stems from the variations in the height of the tropopause according to location in the world and/or the season.

In the UK, reasonable approximations in feet could be as shown in Table 8.5.

Table 8.5

	Low	**Medium**	**High**
Summer	5000	16,000	25,000
Winter	1000	6500	16,000

Within these broad classifications there are particular types, and these are detailed on the following pages.

Types of Cloud

Low Cloud
Stratus (St)

– A layer or sheet of cloud of varying thickness which is sometimes associated with drizzle or light rain.

– Stratus in the early morning during summer will usually herald a good day as soon as the sun can burn it away.

– In winter it can persist all day and produce the condition known as 'Anticyclonic Gloom'.

– Fog is Stratus whose base is at ground level.

Nimbo-Stratus (N St)

– A dense sheet of amorphous-shaped layer cloud whose thickness can extend up into medium cloud levels.

– It is associated with continuous rain preceding a warm front.

Fracto-Nimbus (F Nim)

- The air below Nimbo-Stratus can become saturated by the rain passing through it and it condenses into ragged fragments of cloud often referred to as 'scud cloud'.

Strato-Cumulus (St Cu)

- Patches of cloud, 'lumpy' in appearance but with no great thickness or particular shape.

- It is not indicative of any particular weather.

- It can produce light rain if thick enough when associated with certain types of front.

Small Cumulus (Cu)

- Small puffy cloud whose base is always flat and the top is rounded.

- The length of the base is greater than the height.

- Also known as 'Fair Weather Cloud'.

Large Cumulus (Cu)

- A cumulus cloud whose height exceeds the width of the base. Easily recognisable as towering cloud with 'cauliflower'-shaped tops.

- As long as the tops are crisp in outline it is still active. Once they become ragged then growth has stopped.

- Large Cumulus produce showers which can be heavy or light according to the size of the cloud.

- The tops can extend up into medium cloud levels above.

Cumulo-Nimbus (Cb)

- These are large cumulus which have climbed into the high cloud levels where the tops become ice crystals known as 'false cirrus'.

- The top of a Cu-Nimb is very distinctive as it spreads out in an anvil shape on hitting the invisible roof of equilibrium (of which more will be said later). The anvil moves downwind faster than the rest of the cloud as the winds at the upper level are usually stronger.

- Violent weather is normally associated with this cloud and certainly no microlight should be in the air when it is around.

- Thunderstorms, hail, heavy rain and squalls are all products of these clouds.

- Surface winds can alter to a considerable extent in terms and direction in their vicinity producing wind shear effect.

- May be associated with cold fronts where the warm air being undercut is unstable. They can often be hidden by other cloud formed in the warm sector set up by the warm front that passed previously.

- They are more likely to be found in an unstable polar maritime airstream or at the breakdown of a heat wave.

Mammatus (Mamma)

- Forms under the anvil of a Cu-Nimb or Alto-Cumulus.

- They appear as 'inverted cumulus' with an udder-like shape.

Medium Cloud
Alto-Cumulus (Ac)

- Is Strato-Cumulus at medium height level (Above 6500 ft).

- At times it can form into a pattern known as a 'Mackerel sky'.

Alto-Cumulus Cumulus Genitus (AcCu-CuGen)

– Alto-Cumulus formed by large cumulus spreading out on reaching equilibrium (more later).

– Can cover a large area of the sky thus cutting off the sun's rays and so reducing thermal activity.

– On occasions it can develop into mammatus.

Alto-Stratus (A St)

– Stratus at medium height level.

– Should it appear to be lowering and thickening from the west there is very probably a warm front on the way bringing Nimbo-Stratus and rain.

Alto-Cumulus Lenticularis (Ac Lent)

– Cigar-shaped, medium cloud formed by standing waves in the lee of mountain ranges.

– Lenticular clouds do not move with the wind across the sky like other clouds. They appear at the crest of each wave.

Alto-Cumulus Castellanus (Ac Cast)

– This is a form of Alto-Cumulus which usually appears after a very hot spell. It is distinctive by its hard turreted outline.

– It is a warning that unstable thundery conditions are developing and could break out in a day or so.

– Can appear and disappear several times prior to the thundery outbreaks occurring.

High Cloud
Cirrus (Ci)

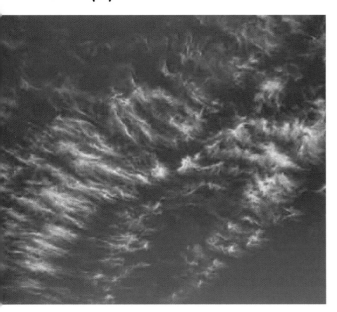

- Due to the freezing temperatures at their height, Cirrus type clouds are composed of ice crystals.

- A fibrous-looking cloud, the most well known form being known as 'Mares' Tails' – streaks which turn up at one end.

Cirro-Stratus (Ci St)

- Stratus at high level.

- If seen thickening and lowering into Alto-Stratus in the west, it is the first sign of a warm front on its way.

Cirro-Cumulus (Ci Cu)

- Similar to Alto-Cumulus in looks but usually composed of ice crystals or ice particles.

- Also forms the 'Mackerel sky' pattern.

- Usually associated with quiet weather.

A sketch of cloud types can be found in Figure 8.32 on page 129.

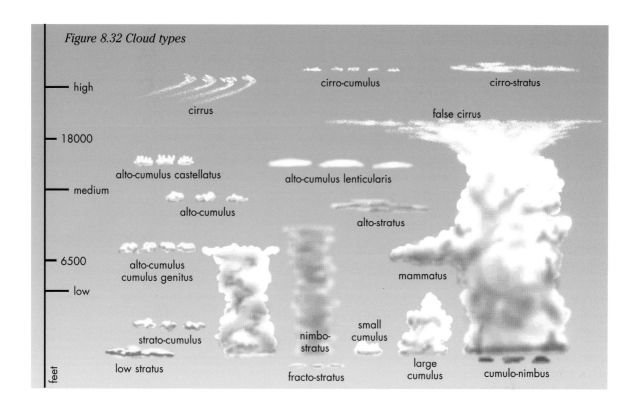

Figure 8.32 Cloud types

high

cirrus

cirro-cumulus

cirro-stratus

false cirrus

18000

alto-cumulus castellatus

alto-cumulus lenticularis

medium

alto-cumulus

alto-stratus

6500

alto-cumulus
cumulus genitus

mammatus

low

strato-cumulus

nimbo-stratus

small cumulus

low stratus

fracto-stratus

large cumulus

cumulo-nimbus

feet

The Forming of Cloud

Referring back to relative humidity, you will recall that when a mass of air was cooled to its dew point temperature, the water vapour content became 100% and any further cooling resulted in condensation into visible water particles, given that condensation nuclei were present of course.

To establish how cloud is formed is simply a matter of examining the various ways in which a mass of air can be cooled to its dew point.

We will look at three different ways in which this can be brought about.

Convection

Easily the most fascinating way in which cloud can be formed, certainly the most important from the point of view of the sailplane and hang glider pilot fraternity from whom we are not too far removed.

Convection is triggered off by causing a mass of air to become warmer than its surround. One method by which this can come about was touched upon in 'Wind Effect', namely that of

uneven heating. Recall the analogy of the rock outcrop and the grass on a hot summer day.

Different substances have varying capacities for heat and the measurement of such capacity is in terms of specific heat. This is the amount of heat required to raise the temperature of a given unit of substance by one degree.

As an example of varying specific heats, take water and copper. An equal amount of heat applied to a unit of water to raise its temperature by 1° would raise the temperature of an equivalent unit of copper by 11°.

Hence you can see how the same amount of sunshine falling on different surfaces will raise their temperature according to the specific heat value of the substance of which each surface is composed.

However, our concern is with the effect of uneven heating rather than its cause.

Air in immediate contact with a surface warmer than surrounding surfaces will itself become warmer than the surrounding air. On warming, it will become less dense than its environment, will break away and rise (Figure 8.33).

Figure 8.33

We must now take into account the different lapse rates discussed earlier as they are the key to what takes place in this situation.

First there is the lapse rate of the atmosphere which is in a state of change from time to time and place to place – hence the regular readings that have to be taken as described earlier to update the **Environmental Lapse Rate (ELR)** as it is called.

Then we have the Dry Adiabatic Lapse Rate which is a constant 3°C (5.4°F) per 1000 ft (DALR). Air forced to rise within its surround will cool at this rate.

An example of what could take place is thus (Figure 8.34).

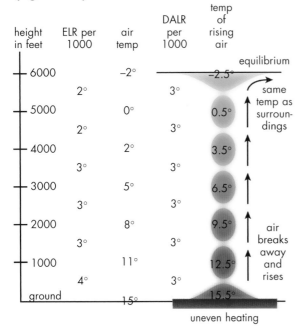

Figure 8.34 (temperatures in degrees Celsius)

In the foregoing example where the ELR is greater than the DALR conditions are said to be **unstable**.

Had the ELR been less than the DALR the warmer air on trying to rise would have quickly become cooler than its surround and would have fallen back to the surface before gaining any height; conditions would have been said to have been **stable** (Figure 8.35).

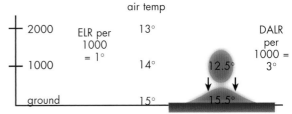

Figure 8.35 (temperatures in degrees Celsius)

We must now consider what happens when the rising air reaches Dew Point level – the level where the temperature is such that the water vapour can condense into water particles.

Remember, as condensation takes place latent heat is given off which effectively reduces the cooling rate of the rising air by half – certainly up to 6000 ft. The cooling rate in the cloud now becomes that of the Saturated Adiabatic Lapse Rate at 1.5°C (2.7°F) per 1000 ft (SALR).

The cloud produced by convection is of the Cumulus type and, with the reduction in cooling due to latent heat, the height which Cumulus clouds reach can be very great indeed before equilibrium comes about (Figure 8.36 on page 131).

Thermal Lift

It is appropriate to digress here for a moment from what convection is to what convection can do for pilots. At the beginning it was said that convection was certainly important to glider and hang glider enthusiasts. The reason is simple – convection brings about rising air and use can be made of this as it is in hill lift.

Unlike hill lift the rising air in convection is not a broad expanse related to a geographical feature; it is in fact a 'column' in shape and is known as a **Thermal**. Many microlight aircraft are quite capable of making use of thermals.

If a thermal ascends at say 1200 ft per minute (FPM) and your sink rate is 600 FPM then by

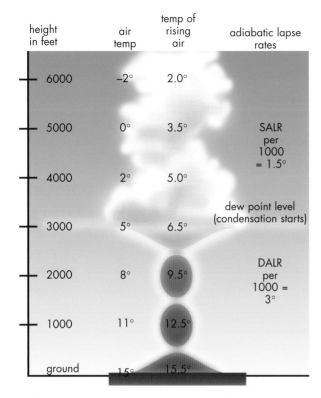

height in feet	air temp	temp of rising air	adiabatic lapse rates
6000	−2°	2.0°	
5000	0°	3.5°	SALR per 1000 = 1.5°
4000	2°	5.0°	
			dew point level (condensation starts)
3000	5°	6.5°	
2000	8°	9.5°	DALR per 1000 = 3°
1000	11°	12.5°	
ground	15°	15.5°	

Figure 8.36 (temperatures in degrees Celsius)

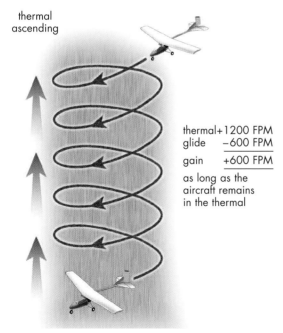

thermal ascending

thermal +1200 FPM
glide   −600 FPM
gain   +600 FPM

as long as the aircraft remains in the thermal

aircraft descending through thermal

Figure 8.37

remaining in the core of the thermal you will gain height relative to the ground at the rate of 600 FPM (Figure 8.37).

Eventually you will glide out of the bottom of the thermal and will have to start the process again with another thermal. Because the thermal is a column, keeping in the core requires correct circling which can only come with experience unless you have access to a two-seater and an instructor to pass on the 'know-how'.

There are some 'wrinkles' for recognising thermals. In level flight or a steady glide you suddenly feel a surge of airspeed and a feeling like being on a boat which is lifted bodily by a wave.

If you have a vertical speed indicator or variometer (a sensitive VSI) you will notice that they register ascent at that moment.

At this moment you have to circle to left or right in an endeavour to keep within the thermal's core where the lift is greatest. If on first sensing the lift you experienced a wing being lifted up, then it is fair to assume that the core lies towards the wing that was affected and you would turn accordingly in that direction.

Before you can recognise a thermal you have to be astute enough to detect likely sources. The most likely places would be rock outcrops, villages, or dry sandy surfaces followed by vegetation covered land with little or no activity over water.

An obvious solution is to fly under any developing Cumulus clouds but if there are no clouds then watch other aircraft or birds. If they look to be on the up and up, go in and join their circle. Having said this, the comparatively poor visibility from some microlights in an upward direction demands that you do this with extreme care.

Another solution is to question pilots as to where they feel the good thermal sources are to be found in that locality. However, you must remember that when a thermal breaks away it travels horizontally with the wind as well as upwards. In all but dead calm conditions its

Figure 8.38

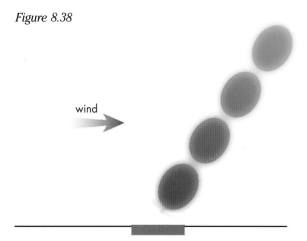

path will always be a slope (Figure 8.38).

So much for the digression. Reverting back to the ways in which cloud can be formed we come to another condition.

Orographic Cloud

Air on meeting mountains rises to pass over them. As it does so it will cool adiabatically and condense if dew point level is reached.

Two types of cloud will basically be the outcome of any condensation that takes place depending on the ELR at the same time. Both will be said to be **orographic**.

– Stratiform cloud in the form of Stratus or Strato-Cumulus if conditions are stable. Such cloud forming below the hill top is designated hill fog.

– Cumiliform cloud if the conditions are unstable and convection is triggered off by the rising air.

Examples are shown in Figure 8.39.

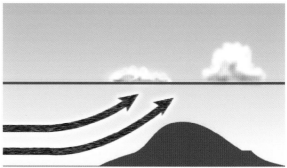

Figure 8.39

You will recall that mountain ranges can set up standing waves. Just as such ranges can produce cloud in their proximity so the waves that are created can do likewise.

Where dew point level is just below the crest of the wave, the air travelling up to the crest cools and condenses producing cloud. This cloud will immediately evaporate as the air warms up on travelling down the other side of the crest.

The clouds so produced are of a most distinctive shape known as Lenticular clouds. They lie across the wind and can exist for great distances downwind of the mountain range that caused them (Figure 8.40).

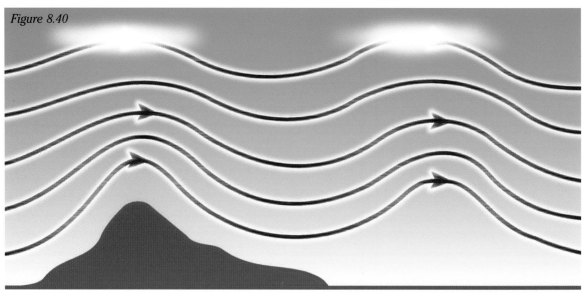

Figure 8.40

They are usually at medium cloud level, are cigar-like in shape and easily recognisable because they do not move with the wind; they remain stationary at the crest.

Being at medium height they are probably only of academic interest to the microlight pilot. On the other hand, wave effect can be experienced in the lower levels so they could be taken as indicative of wave effect being about.

To the sailplane pilot they are a veritable signpost to standing waves and subsequent distance goals.

Now to the remaining cause of cloud.

Air Masses

An air mass is no more than its name implies – a mass of air. It is its characteristics that are important and these are acquired from the region of the earth's surface over which it forms.

Such regions are known as **source regions** and they are usually associated with the centre of a slow moving anticyclone; where the stable conditions allow the air to stagnate and absorb the characteristics of the source region.

As the main anticyclone belts are to be found in the polar and tropical latitudes of the world, it will not come as a surprise to know that there are two basic types of air mass – polar and tropical. But the distinction does not stop there.

Where stagnation takes place over land, the air will be relatively dry whilst over sea areas it will become moist due to evaporation.

This produces two further sub-types of air mass – dry, known as continental, and moist, known as maritime (Figure 8.41).

We thus end up with four main types:

Polar Maritime – Cold/Moist
Polar Continental – Cold/Dry
Tropical Maritime – Warm/Moist
Tropical Continental – Warm/Dry

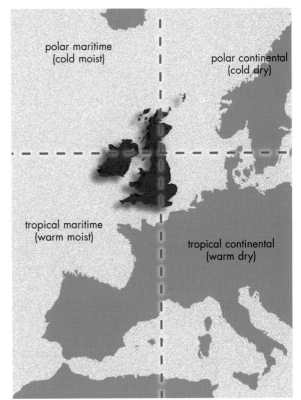

Figure 8.41

As you can see the British Isles lies in a 'Pig in the Middle' situation in that they all too frequently experience the influence of all four types of air mass. Because of this they lend themselves to being a good subject for the study of weather. No doubt their geographical position has led to the old adage – 'the climate in Britain is really quite pleasant – it's the weather that's so b..... awful!'

When one pressure system (a high or a low) gains dominance over another, air from the air mass begins to travel. This is known as an **Airstream**. Note: at times the word Airmass is used to mean Airstream as well.

En route it will take on any different characteristics it finds by changes in the surface over which it passes. This process is known as **Transformation**. Naturally the extent of transformation depends not only on the differing surfaces over which it travels but also the length of time it takes to do so.

An excellent example of transformation sometimes takes place in proximity to the British Isles when a large depression – or low – is centred to the west and a polar maritime airstream is heading south (Figure 8.42).

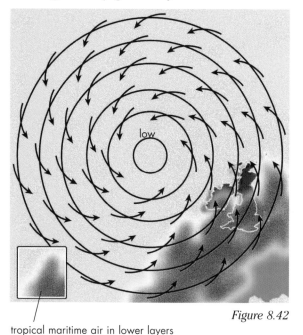

tropical maritime air in lower layers

Figure 8.42

The air mass can be moved sufficiently far south to take up tropical characteristics from the warmer seas – at least tropic in characteristics in the lower layers.

When this situation arises the airstream is known as a **Returning Polar Maritime** airstream (airmass).

Any polar maritime airstream will always undergo a measure of transformation on moving south over a relatively warmer sea though not maybe to the extent in the example above.

However, the journey over sea may be shorter with little or no opportunity to warm up. This occurs when a polar maritime airstream comes down on to the British Isles directly from the north. The result is a really cold blast indeed and such a flow is known as an **Arctic Maritime** airstream (airmass).

The various airstreams in relation to the pressure centres responsible for their movement are shown in Figure 8.43 below.

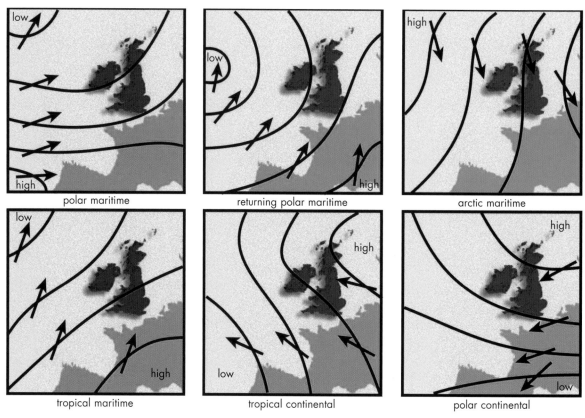

polar maritime

returning polar maritime

arctic maritime

tropical maritime

tropical continental

polar continental

Figure 8.43

CHAPTER 8

Fronts

The British Isles once again present themselves as a good example for our next discussion, lying as they do at the approximate meeting point of the Arctic Low and Tropical High pressure belts depicted in Figure 8.7 on page 110.

As one or the other of these belts gains dominance at a given time so the systems caused (Highs, Lows, etc.) move the differing air masses into contact with each other. The meeting point in this 'battle zone' is known as a **front**, where a 'kink' can occur as warm air makes an incursion into the cold air (Figure 8.44).

Figure 8.44

Fronts are normally associated with depressions which usually move from west to east. They appear on a weather map thus (Figure 8.45).

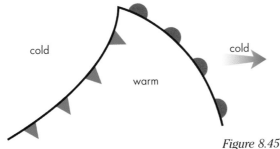

Figure 8.45

The warm front moves faster than the cold air before it and being warmer (less dense) it climbs up over it. The following cold front slowly overtakes the warm air but being colder (more dense) it undercuts it and forces it up. A cross-section at ground level would look thus (Figure 8.46).

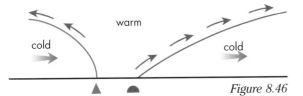

Figure 8.46

When the cold air finally overtakes the warm air the front is said to have been 'occluded' (Figure 8.47).

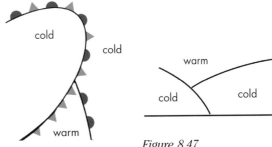

Figure 8.47

It was said earlier that fronts are normally associated with depressions. A picture of how the relationship would appear on a chart is shown in Figure 8.48.

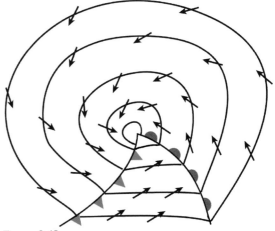

Figure 8.48

Notice in particular how the fronts cause a 'kink' in the isobars – there can be a distinct veer in the wind as a front passes.

Clouds Associated with Fronts

Fronts are capable of producing most of the cloud types listed.

At a front it is the warm air which is predominantly responsible for the formation of cloud, as it can contain so much more water vapour than the colder air.

Cloud is formed by:

– Warm air cooling on climbing over relatively colder air (warm front).

– Warm air cooling on rising at being undercut by relatively colder air (cold front).

Figure 8.49 The 'textbook' frontal situation

In the cold sector as cold wet air comes down from the North West the bottom of the mass is warmed and convection sets in to produce cumulus of all types with showers.

The cold front being denser sharply undercuts the warm air causing a short spell of heavy rain, squalls or even thunder. A further veer of wind.

The situation depicted is known as a 'classical' cold front and presupposes the warm air is unstable.

As the warm front goes through the rain slackens off and shapeless nimbo-stratus becomes stratus and strato-cumulus. The wind veers with the passing of the front. Drizzle may occur.

Continuous rain from lowering nimbo-stratus – can go on for some hours depending on speed of front.

Cirro-stratus has lowered to form alto-stratus and rain may be visible far to the West. Little or no low cloud will be present.

Cirrus in the West thickens into cirro-stratus as warm air climbs up over the colder air. Any convection cloud begins to die out.

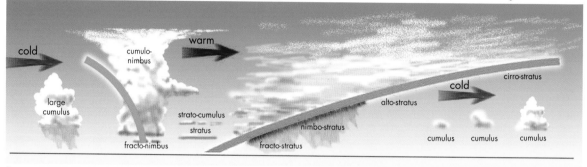

Pressure continues to rise.

Pressure starts to rise.

Pressure drop eases or levels off.

Pressure drop continues. Rate of drop shows the intensity of the depression.

Pressure begins to drop.

A 'text book' picture of a classical warm and cold front cloud situation is shown in Figure 8.49.

Would that life was like Figure 8.49; prediction would be so simple. Unfortunately textbook situations are like average situations – they rarely occur.

The atmosphere is usually in constant motion – wind is a perfect example of this in the horizontal sense. There is also a vertical motion but the speed is not even remotely the same as wind.

This particular vertical motion is distinctly separate from convection.

You will recall that cloud is formed by rising air, cooling as it does so, and condensing at dew point level. Conversely, when air descends, it warms, can contain more moisture and therefore disperses cloud or precludes it from forming.

It is this albeit very slow vertical motion up or down which causes the formation or dispersal of most types of layer cloud at all levels.

So how does this affect our 'textbook' fronts?

Should there be a descending movement in the warm air at a front, the depth to which the cloud extends will be stunted.

Compared with the warm front depicted in Figure 8.49, the picture will be more like this (Figure 8.50).

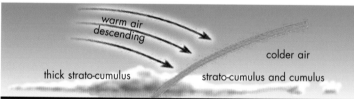

Figure 8.50 Kata Warm Front

The above type of front is called a **Kata Warm Front**.

Earlier when we discussed wind we talked about Katabatic and Anabatic winds. The former descended down the hill whilst the latter blew up it. Hence, in describing a front we call it a Kata warm front if warm air is descending and an Ana warm front if it is ascending.

The 'textbook' warm front in Figure 8.49 is an **Ana Warm Front**. The cloud depth is very great due to the warm moist air ascending without restraint to high cloud (Cirrus) levels.

Cold fronts are also affected by whether the warm air is descending or ascending as it is undercut by colder air. You can therefore have Kata or Ana cold fronts.

In a **Kata Cold Front**, once again the depth of cloud is minimised by the descending warm air (Figure 8.51).

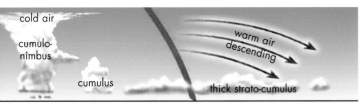

Figure 8.51 Kata Cold Front

Finally we are left with the **Ana Cold Front** to complete the picture – that is, colder air under-cutting ascending warm air.

This form of front manifests itself in two distinct ways according to whether the warm air is unstable or not.

If the air is unstable then you will see the classical cold front produced. This is shown in Figure 8.49.

However, in Britain such a situation seldom arises as warm air masses are rarely unstable. Also, the warm air is usually descending.

If the warm air is stable the picture is simply the reverse of the Ana warm front in Figure 8.49, except the width of the front is around only one-third to one-half of the warm front belt (Figure 8.52).

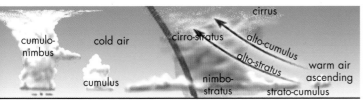

Figure 8.52 Ana Cold Front

The Ana cold front in Figure 8.52 does occur in Britain but mostly during the winter months.

There is one distinctive feature common to both types of Ana cold front. The rear edge of the associated cloud mass is very clear-cut, particularly at high levels. In fact it can appear as a virtual straight line right across the sky.

The demarcation of weather types is also more clearly defined – as is the transition from warm to cold air and the veer in wind direction.

Kata fronts are less vigorous in terms of weather and rainfall amounts – be they warm or cold. Also, all the changes just elaborated upon are much slower in taking place and are more ill-defined.

To sum up, no two fronts are ever likely to be exactly the same – neither will be the clouds associated with them.

However, from a flying point of view they must be treated with caution. Unless a front is very weak, rainfall, low cloud and poor visibility are a racing certainty. Poor visibility is particularly hazardous as not only can it hide hills but, as a warm front passes, it could mean you are less likely to spot that very dangerous unstable cold front that could be lurking in the offing.

Always be prepared to abandon your plans to fly. It is better to be on the ground wishing you were in the air than to be in the air wishing to heaven you were on the ground!

Weather

Normally you would not be flying in 'weather' as it is referred to here. Nevertheless there is always the need for understanding as much about the sky as possible when you are 'hooked' on taking the odd excursion into it.

Rain

–When condensation continues to produce more and more water particles they join up to become larger in size until finally they are too heavy for the rising currents in the cloud to support them. They fall in the form of rain.

–Should the ability to hold them up be too weak before they become as large as rain drops, they will fall before reaching any size at all – this is known as drizzle. The official distinction between rain and drizzle is quite simple. Rain will make a splash in a puddle; drizzle will not.

Hail

– In Cumulo-Nimbus cloud the up currents are so powerful that not only can very large drops be sustained but they are taken up to very great heights – often several times before leaving the cloud. At the heights they reach they freeze and fall as drops of ice called hail.

Snow

– When condensation takes place below freezing point the water vapour changes directly into ice crystals. When these crystals join up and become heavy enough they fall as snow.–A mixture of rain and snow is known as sleet.

Fog

– Fog is Stratus at ground level and is a great hazard to pilots in flight. Internationally, fog is said to exist when visibility falls below 1 km; but in the UK the official figure is 200 yards (180 metres) before any public warning is issued.

– There are basically two types of fog:

Radiation Fog

– After sunset when no further heating of the earth's surface can take place, if the sky is cloudless the heat stored rapidly radiates into the atmosphere and the surface quickly cools. The air in contact with the cold surface will also cool and if the relative humidity is very high not much will be required to meet dew point and thus condensation.

– In summer the longer days see the surface storing so much heat that it is not finally cool enough to cause condensation in the air until around dawn – hence early morning mists.

– In winter the heat received is much less so the cooling time to dew point is much less – hence fog shortly after sunset. Radiation fog requires a light wind to trigger it off but will not form when a reasonable wind is blowing. The stronger wind mixes the air and prevents a well defined cooling at the surface with low Stratus being formed rather than fog.

Advection Fog

– This is caused when a warm air mass passes over a colder surface; it is particularly prevalent at sea. If such a mass moves into a region of colder sea the lower levels of the air mass are cooled and they condense into fog banks.

– Fog banks normally disperse if blown inland as the warmer land evaporates the fog back into water vapour. However, if the land happens to be as cold then the fog will remain. In winter when the sea is relatively warmer than the land – particularly at night – any fog moving off the land will disperse on contact with the sea.

General

– If the strength of the sun is sufficient all types of fog will burn away after a time. If complete dispersal is not effected the fog may lift from the ground and remain as low Stratus.

– Fog is predictable given that one knows the temperature and relative humidity at the time.

– Great care should be taken in flying at sunset during autumn and winter when skies are clear; radiation fog can quite suddenly form and catch you napping.

Thunder

– Thunderstorms occur in fully developed Cu-Nimb clouds and have the habit of fascinating people or scaring them silly – there seems to be no happy medium.

– Large water droplets can form in the vigorous upcurrents, freeze, and can equally be broken down by them, leading to them becoming positively electrified. The air becomes charged and eventually when large amounts of electricity accumulate a lightning flash occurs.

– 'Forked' lightning is the visible sign of a discharge from cloud to earth.

– 'Sheet' lightning is the discharge from cloud to cloud where the flash is diffused by the cloud.

– The noise which follows a lightning flash is set up by the sudden heating and expansion of the air followed by an equally rapid cooling and contraction.

– A rough estimate of the distance a thunderstorm is away from you is to allow a mile for every five seconds between flash and noise.

Weather is very much associated with pressure systems. Naturally the intensity of the weather will be related to the intensity of the system.

Depression (Low)

- Bad weather with continuous rain, high winds and low cloud. Usually associated with fronts. Winds veer as each front passes.

Trough

- Similar to a depression but not so long-lasting.

Col

- Neutral weather. If a high lapse rate exists with a high relative humidity there will be a tendency towards thundery conditions.

Anticyclone (High)

- Good weather, dry, often bringing cloudless skies in winter and summer.

- In winter the air will be colder and the relative humidity higher, therefore cloud is more likely to form. This will burn away or not burn away according to the thickness of the cloud layer and the strength of the sun at the time.

- When a really thick layer exists during the quiet period of a High it gives rise to exceptional dullness known as 'Anticyclonic Gloom'.

- Air in a High is basically stable and no convection to speak about is usually present. This gives rise to hazy conditions in summer with the likelihood of anything from mist to thick fog in winter.

- Visibility is certainly a problem during these conditions especially when flying up sun.

Ridge

- Period of settled weather between two poor spells.

Icing

We will start with a few points on ice itself. Just as condensation nuclei is a prerequisite for condensation to take place, so there is a need for **freezing nuclei** to be present for ice to form.

The process of transforming water vapour into ice crystals is known chemically as deposition but in meteorological circles it is referred to as **sublimation**.

Without the presence of freezing nuclei, water droplets can remain in liquid form well under 0°C. They are then known as **super-cooled** droplets or particles (depending on size) but they will usually turn to ice on striking an object.

Such droplets, lifted up to cirrus level in a cunimb cloud can transform into ice crystals by the process known as **glaciation**.

And so on to the forms of icing that can relate to aviation.

Hoar Frost

- Ice crystals formed by sublimation onto a cold surface with a temperature below 0°C. It can occur on an aircraft when parked or when descending from below freezing level into warmer moister air. Such frost or any similar deposit must be removed totally from an aircraft prior to flight. Not only does it add extra weight but it can jeopardise lift by distorting the smooth flow of air over the wing.

Rime Ice

- Flight through cloud with a relatively low moisture content containing super-cooled water particles can produce rime ice as the particles freeze on striking the aircraft. The icing will be in the form of a white opaque deposit confined to the leading edge of the wing and its immediate surround (Figure 8.53). As it builds up the airflow can begin to break it away but sufficient can remain to disturb the smooth airflow over the wing, affecting lift and thereby the stall speed.

Figure 8.53

- Rime ice is usually associated with stratiform cloud where the super-cooled particles are small.

Clear Ice

- Also called **glazed ice**, this is the most hazardous form of all. When an aircraft is flying through dense towering cu and cu-nimb cloud it will be striking very large super-cooled droplets indeed.

- Initially, on striking the aircraft, only *part* of the droplet will freeze instantly for the following reason. Recall how latent heat is given off when condensation takes place; so, further latent heat is released when a liquid changes into a solid. This heat delays total freezing of the droplet momentarily, thus enabling the still liquid part of the droplet to flow back over a wing (or other flying surface).

- Although it will virtually freeze as it flows it will now be covering a much larger area and with repetition of the process, as more droplets strike the aircraft, the aerofoil shape of the wing can be severely distorted to a much greater extent than it would be by rime ice – not to mention the additional weight. This **ice accretion** as it is called will have a major detrimental, in fact dangerous, effect on the aircraft's handling and stall speed.

Rain Ice

- Similar to clear or glazed ice but on this occasion the aircraft will be flying in sub-zero temperature *outside* cloud but through rain falling from relatively warmer moist air above.

- Should the raindrops become super-cooled in falling through the freezing temperature they will freeze on striking the already sub-zero surface of the aircraft (Figure 8.54).

Summary

Meteorology can be a very complex subject but the foregoing in its relatively simplistic state should be sufficient for your immediate needs.

However, in the Introduction it was stressed that you should in no way simply study meteorology for the sake of passing your examination. It is a very changeable element with which you must keep abreast throughout your flying life.

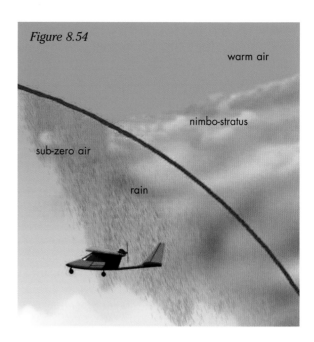

Figure 8.54

warm air

nimbo-stratus

sub-zero air

rain

To this end, after you have obtained that precious licence, my book *Pilot's Weather* will help you delve that little bit deeper into the machinations of weather and will do so with similar simplicity but enhanced with copious illustrations of the clouds and weather systems you must learn to read from the sky. Yes, this is a commercial – for your own sake!

Sources of Aviation Forecasts

Apart from knowledge you may have gained through the pages read in this chapter you should always pay due attention to the official weather forecasts and charts available. They will not only be those for the public from TV stations and newspapers; more importantly for you as a pilot are those related to aviation which can be obtained by online web services or telephone.

There are a host of various weather reports and forecasts available to you – some in plain language such as AIRMET and others in code such as a METAR and TAF.

As they can undergo amendment, or be added to in number from time to time, they are not dealt with in detail in this book. A full presentation of these sources and any codes involved is to be found in an excellent booklet from the Met Office called – *Get Met.*

Copies of this free booklet may be obtained from:

Met Office
FitzRoy Road
Exeter
Devon
EX1 3PB
Fax 0870 900 5050
Email: aviation@metoffice.gov.uk
www.metoffice.gov.uk/aviation

It is acknowledged that the modern microlight now has the capability to travel further than its predecessor of early days. Nevertheless, the journeys are still mainly from one microlight site to another. They are not necessarily to defined aerodromes used by other types of aircraft – aerodromes where the coded current weather report such as the METAR and the forecast such as the TAF are available for intending visitors.

You should at least become familiar with the existence of METARs and TAFs as you may be flying to a site not far from a reporting airfield where you decide it would be worthwhile to seek the information from them. However, in doing so take into account any hills, mountains and costal factors in the area; they can dramatically affect weather conditions between two locations only a few miles apart.

In *Get Met* there are telephone numbers for obtaining help when you find it difficult to understand or access the available information. For those requiring special information it is possible to consult with a forecaster. This service currently costs £21 including VAT – payable by credit card. The fee does not cover the cost of the phone call.

It is essential you obtain a copy of *Get Met* to use in conjunction with the meteorological section in this book. Questions on the sources of aviation weather information may be asked in your meteorology examination paper. Ensure your copy is up to date; it is reviewed anually for any necessary amendments with a new edition usually available by late January. Between editions of *Get Met*, frequently check the index page relevant to the service required; also, any such changes can usually be found in an **Aeronautical Information Circular (AIC)** issued by the CAA.

ISA Data

Table 8.6

Pressure at MSL	1013.25 hPa
Altimeter Setting	1013.2 hPa
Temperature at MSL	15° Celsius
Average lapse Rate (to 36,000 ft)	–2°C per 1000 ft (–1.98°C to be precise)
Density	1225 g/m³

Note: With density not being measurable in the same manner as pressure or temperature, you must therefore **remember that –**

A density *decrease* comes about with:

– a pressure *decrease* and/or

– a temperature *increase* and/or

– a relative humidity *increase*

A density *increase* will come about when each of the above occurrences are reversed.

Chapter 9
Navigation

Introduction

Navigation and map reading are often associated with each other in aviation textbooks. However, in this book the accent is on microlight aeroplanes and navigation may be considered by pilots of microlights to be irrelevant.

'There is no way I can plot on charts when exposed to a 50 to 60 knots airstream rushing past' – is often the natural retort to the suggestion of navigation under these circumstances.

Because of the limitations imposed by microlight flight the two subjects must be looked at thus:

- **Navigation** is **planning** your way from A to B **prior to** flight.

- **Map reading** is **finding** your way from A to B **during** flight.

With regard to the former, the serious navigator uses charts devoid of all detail other than the lines of latitude and longitude and certain major features. There is therefore plenty of room for pencilled plots and calculations, all of which will be clearly legible.

In a microlight, plotting charts will never enter the picture – basically you will find yourself confined to the use of aeronautical maps and with the wealth of detail thereon little room will be found for anything but the barest of calculations.

In actual fact, you will find that any calculations you may choose to make can be quite easily carried out on a sheet of plain paper.

Position Plot

Establishing your position on a map or chart is a natural pre-requisite for navigating.

The earth is divided up into segments by lines of latitude and longitude which run as follows:

Latitude
- Lines at 1° intervals running parallel to the north and south of the Equator ranging from 0° to 90° N or S.

Longitude
- Lines at 1° intervals running east and west of a line running from the North to the South Pole which passes through Greenwich. This base line is known as the Greenwich Meridian and longitude is measured in a range of 0° to 180° E or W of Greenwich (See Figure 9.1).

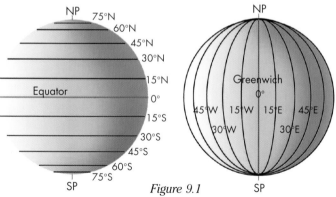

Figure 9.1

Degrees of latitude and longitude are broken down into 'minutes' with 60 minutes equal to 1 degree.

A position can therefore be given for any place in the world expressed as degrees/minutes north or south of the Equator and east or west of the Greenwich Meridian.

In terms of distance, 1 minute is equal to 1 nautical mile (nm) which in turn is equal to one and one-seventh statute miles along lines of latitude.

Where longitude is concerned a minute of latitude can only equal 1 nm along the Equator. North or south of this latitude the lines of longitude converge on the poles progressively narrowing as they do so.

Compass Readings

Compass readings are in degrees from 001° to 360°.

There is a discrepancy between the geographical north (**True North**) and the direction in which a compass needle will point (**Magnetic North**). The angle is known as **Variation**. This angle can vary both with time and with position on the Earth's surface. Lines joining places of equal variation are known as **Isogonals** – they will be shown on your maps and indicate the value, the effective date as well as the rate of change.

A further complication is caused by magnetic fields created by aircraft themselves as described in the previous chapter. The further difference between the magnetic north and the direction in which the compass needle points (**Compass North**) is the angle known as **Deviation**.

In navigation all bearings or headings are related to **True North** (the Geographical North) so to establish a **Compass Heading [Hdg(C)]** which will provide a required **True Heading [Hdg(T)]** there are a few minor calculations to be made.

Variation and deviation can be either east or west, a situation which can be confusing unless some form of 'jingle' is remembered to help avoid mistakes. It is this:

> 'Variation West – Magnetic Best' –
> Add to True Heading
>
> 'Variation East – Magnetic Least' –
> Subtract from True Heading.

The same jingle applies to deviation but for 'magnetic' read 'compass'. Remember, variation is applied to **True** headings and deviation

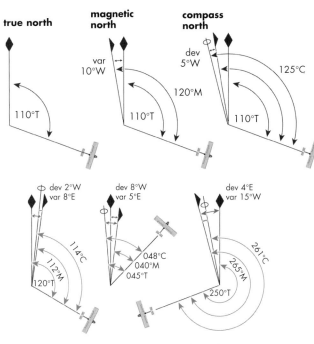

Figure 9.2 Note symbols for types of North

to **Magnetic** headings. Examples can be found in Figure 9.2.

Table 9.1 contains some examples for you to work out. (The answers may be found at the end of the chapter.)

Table 9.1

	Hdg (T)	Var	Hdg (M)	Dev	Hdg (C)
(i)	102°	10°W		3°E	
(ii)	224°	8°W		2°W	
(iii)	049°	5°E		1°W	
(iv)		3°W		2°E	164°
(v)		6°E	331°	4°W	
(vi)	140°		145°		143°

Navigational Instruments

A limited number of simple instruments are required for solving navigational problems 'by hand' for the want of a better term.

Protractor

- For measuring headings against lines of longitude.

Navigational Rule

- For measuring distance in nautical or statute miles. The scale of the rule must match that of the map. An ordinary ruler used in conjunction with the scale on the map will suffice if nothing else is to hand.

Dividers/Compasses

- For transporting measurements from the rule on to your working.

Manual and electronic computers are available for carrying out all navigational problems – their use is a matter of personal choice. Learning to use them is best undertaken by working out examples on the computers themselves as per the makers' instructions rather than attempting to follow diagrams in a book. Also, you could well have to work out answers for yourself in any examination you may take so reliance on mechanical or electronic aids is not such a good thing.

Track and Heading

The line drawn on your map depicting your route from A to B is known as the **Track Required (Tr. Req.)**.

By measuring the angle of the track in relation to a line of longitude you establish the direction you must travel in relation to True North. A line that crosses the meridians of longitude at the same angle is a **rhumb line** and is the track you fly when using a compass. To ensure that you accurately measure the angle of the rhumb line, the protractor should be referenced to a meridian of longitude close to the centre of the track. This will compensate for any distortions resulting from representing the three-dimensional world on a flat map. Assuming there is not wind to be considered, this direction is known as your **True Heading**

[Hdg.(T)] and to this must be applied Variation to establish your **Magnetic Heading [Hdg.(M)]** to ensure that your travel will be along the Tr. Req. in relation to True North.

Deviation must be applied where necessary but as this alters from aircraft to aircraft and also with the direction in which the aircraft happens to be heading, we will from this moment on take it as read and ignore it for the purposes of demonstrating problems.

Timing

If you know the **Airspeed** at which you are going to fly and you know the distance along your track then it is possible to lay down the time your flight will take thus allowing you to state an **Estimated Time of Arrival (ETA)** based on your actual time of departure.

The formula is quite simply:
$$\frac{\text{Distance of Track}}{\text{Airspeed}}$$
ensuring that both inputs are in the same terminology viz. nautical miles or statute miles. Take great care in working out problems to make sure that you never mix the two.

All this is fine in still air but rarely will you come across such conditions.

Effect of Wind

Referring back for a moment to the effect of wind on take-off and landing you will recall that your airspeed for sustaining flight was reached at a lower groundspeed when pointing into wind. Fine for achieving take-off in the shortest possible distance, but a factor to be reckoned with once airborne and wanting to reach your destination in the quickest possible time.

For example, take Figure 9.3:

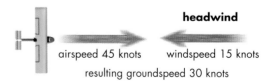

Figure 9.3

On a trip of 90 nautical miles at an airspeed of 45 knots the flight time in still air would be two hours. However, as in Figure 9.3 with the headwind reducing your actual **Groundspeed** to 30 knots the time in air will turn out to be 3 hours.

Should your planned fuel allow for 2½ hours time in air you can see that because of the headwind you will in fact be back on the ground after covering only 75 nautical miles with 15 nautical miles unattained – assuming a 30 knots groundspeed.

Conversely, a tailwind will add to groundspeed for a given airspeed. In the example given, at an airspeed of 45 knots the groundspeed will be 60 knots, thus seeing your 90 nautical mile track being covered in 1½ hours leaving plenty of fuel to spare.

To complicate matters further, just as still air is something of a rarity so is the likelihood of your **Track Required (Tr. Req.)** being precisely upwind or downwind.

Triangle of Velocities

Returning to the water again. A boat intends to cross a river from A to B which is the Tr. Req. However, a current is flowing which will make the boat track from A to C when the heading is set towards B. This resulting track is known as the **Track Made Good (TMG)** (Figure 9.4).

To counteract the current and ensure that the TMG coincides with the Tr. Req. means adopting a **Heading** into the current. If the adjustment is not correct then the *angle* between TMG and Tr. Req. is known as **Track Error**. The angle between the heading and TMG is called **Drift** (Figure 9.5).

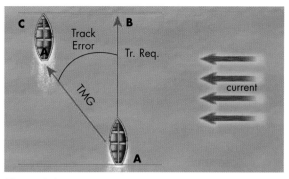

Figure 9.4

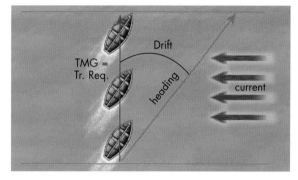

Figure 9.5

In the air a similar adjustment must be made to counteract any drift caused by the wind. This adjustment will always be **into** the windward side of the track.

The exact amount of adjustment is calculated by drawing three **Vectors** to form a **Triangle of Velocities**.

Each vector comprises a velocity related to the flight – a velocity being a speed and a direction.

The three velocities are shown in Table 9.2 below.

Table 9.2

Velocity:	1	2	3
Speed:	**True Airspeed (TAS)** The indicated airspeed corrected for instrument error, temperature and altitude in mph or kt – a kt being 1 nm per hour	**Wind Speed (V)** Wind speed in mph or kt	**Groundspeed (GS)** The speed at which the aircraft travels along the track in relation to the ground – in mph or kt
Direction:	**True Heading [Hdg(T)]** The direction the aircraft is pointing in relation to True North	**Wind Direction (W)** The direction **from** which the wind blows in relation to True North	**Track Required (Tr.Req.)** The direction the aircraft is required to travel over the ground in relation to True North

Given any two of the above vectors the third can always be deduced.

We will now take an example and follow it through.

You wish to go from A to B.

- **Distance** is 60 nm
- **Tr. Req.** is 215° (T)
- **Wind** (W/V) is 140°/15 kt
- **TAS** will be 50 kt

The two unknowns are:

- **Hdg(T)** to counter Drift.
- **GS** resulting from wind effect.

1 With a protractor and a ruler, use a longitude line on your map (or a vertical line on plain paper as per the example) and lay off a line from A to B at 215° True North – the Tr. Req. Mark this line with two arrows (Figure 9.6a)

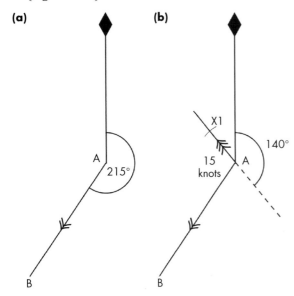

Figure 9.6 (a) & (b)

2 Next, lay off a wind line at 140° *downwind* from start point A. Mark this line with three arrows. Now select a scale which is large enough to allow accuracy and small enough to fit your work surface. To depict the 15 knots wind vector, measure off the dividers to 15 on your scale and outward from A along the wind line intersect with an arc X1 (Figure 9.6b)

3 Next, to depict the 50 knots TAS vector, measure off the dividers to 50 and out from X1 intersect the A to B line with an arc X2 and mark this line with one arrow. The length of line from **A to X2** shows the actual GS will be 44 knots due to the part head-wind (Figure 9.6c)

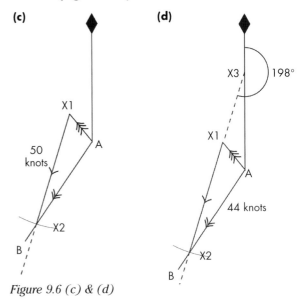

Figure 9.6 (c) & (d)

4 Finally, extend the line back from X2 to X1 to intersect the True North (vertical) line at X3. The **angle of the line** related to True North will give you a Hdg(T) of 198° needed to keep the Tr. Req. (Figure 9.6d).

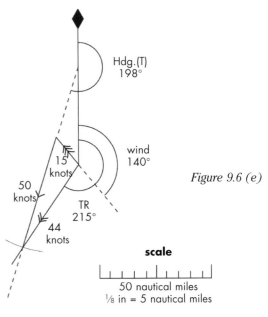

Figure 9.6 (e)

You have now calculated the two unknowns GS and Hdg(T) – the former one shows that your 60 nautical mile journey at 44 knots will take 82 minutes. The working in its entirety is shown in Figure 9.6e.

A few points to remember about the Triangle of Velocities.

– Speed in mph or knots is immaterial as long as they are not mixed in any one calculation.

– The heading and wind arrows should always be following each other around the triangle and be in opposition to the track arrows.

– Think about what you are doing. Try to visualise the way the vectors should be pointing as you consider the problem. For example, in the problem just discussed (Figure 9.6) the wind had a lot of 'head' component in it so obviously GS should work out to be **less** than TAS.

– Also, the Hdg(T) should obviously be **less** than the Tr. Req. by virtue of the rule that adjustment is always **into** wind of track.

– When winds are directly head-on or tail-on to Tr. Req., no triangle is necessary – you simply subtract or add on the windspeed to the TAS to read GS.

A Reciprocal Track

There will be occasions when your flight is an 'out and return'. In other words, the flight home will cover the same ground as the outward path – known as a reciprocal. The reciprocal track will therefore be the outward Tr. Req. plus or minus 180°.

If there is any wind to consider during the planning of your flight it will result in an increase to the combined flight time of the 'out and return' trip. In other words, the longer flight time due to a decrease in groundspeed resulting from a headwind component will not be fully compensated for by the higher groundspeed whilst flying in the opposite direction. So, providing that the wind velocity is constant, the quickest 'out and return' trip will be achieved in calm conditions. The drift experienced, however, will be the same in both directions. You will find that the heading you

require is the *reciprocal of your outward heading* (not track) corrected for *double the drift* experienced on the outward journey.

For example, your outward track was 280° but the heading was 295° to counteract drift of 15° to port. The heading home for the reciprocal Tr. Req. will therefore be 295 – 180 = 115° less (15° × 2) = 085°.

In practice it is usually necessary to work out a new triangle of velocities in order to calculate your groundspeed for the return flight. If, however, the wind is exactly at 90° to the track required, then the groundspeed will be the same in both directions.

The Navigational Computer

Those who work at producing their own triangles of velocities will soon find it to be no problem. However, in this day and age for those of you seeking the easy way out, there are a number of 'computers' around – both manually operated and electronic – which not only solve the one problem but also offer a multitude of additional information.

No doubt it all ends up with 'you pays your money and you takes your choice!' But do make sure the one you settle on meets your requirements.

Correcting Errors *En Route*

No longer as popular as in days gone by, there are two approaches which will be laid to rest in the 'want to know' rather than the 'need to know' category.

The 1-in-60 Rule

Your flight plan prepared on the ground is not working out in the air.

– The Met man was wrong in the winds he gave you.

– You forgot to adjust for variation or deviation.

– You are not flying at the planned airspeed.

– Your compass is out.

The result is that with all your planning you end up having travelled a Track Made Good (TMG) which is not the Tr. Req. Recalculating whilst alone in a microlight exposed to the elements is not very feasible but if you can put up with a modicum of mental arithmetic then help is at hand. The 1-in-60 rule is a better than nothing way to put things right in spite of limitations.

The rule is based on the principle that for every 1 nm off track after travelling 60 nm you will have been 1° out in your heading – there will have been 1° of drift or **Track Error** which is the term used to describe the difference between TMG and Tr. Req.

Thus, Track Error = $\dfrac{\text{(Distance off Track)} \times 60}{\text{(Distance Gone)}}$

or Track Error = $\dfrac{\text{DOT} \times 60}{\text{DG}}$

E.g. On a journey of 100 nm you find yourself 6 nm to starboard of Tr. Req. at point B after travelling 40 nautical miles (Figure 9.7).

Track Error = $\dfrac{6 \times 60}{40}$ = 9° Starboard

Adjusting your heading by 9° to **Port** will stop the drift but leave you on a track parallel to Tr. Req. As your waypoints relate to Tr. Req. it is essential to regain your original track as soon as possible.

The rule is to **double** your track error – in this case making it 18° to Port and this will see your Tr. Req. regained at point C in the same time it took to reach point B.

Remember that on regaining your Tr. Req. you must adjust your heading again by the original track error, that is, 9° Starboard and this will ensure that you maintain Tr. Req. from then on.

This rule also provides you with a time check as well as visual checks to help you establish Tr. Req. once again.

The formula to regain Tr. Req. thus becomes

$\dfrac{2 \times \text{(Distance off Track)} \times 60}{\text{(Distance Gone)}}$

or $\dfrac{2 \times \text{DOT} \times 60}{\text{DG}}$

All simple rules have their limitations and the 1-in-60 Rule is no exception. After you have reached the half way mark of your flight applying the rule will see you regain your original track but **after** your destination has passed.

Some recommend that in this instance you triple your track error and in certain circumstances this works.

A more useful approach at this stage in the flight – certainly if two thirds of it have passed – would be to adjust your heading so that you reach your destination. This would avoid 'zigzagging' which would result in the alternative of adjusting to regain Tr. Req.

To do this the formula is

$$\frac{\text{DOT} \times 60}{\text{DG}} \times \frac{\text{Total Track}}{\text{Dist. to Go}}$$

or $\dfrac{\text{DOT} \times 60}{\text{DG}} \times \dfrac{\text{TTr}}{\text{DTG}}$

E.g. On the 100 nm track you are 6 nm to starboard off that track after travelling 60 nm (Figure 9.8 on page 149).

Adjustment to Destination =

$$\frac{\text{DOT} \times 60}{\text{DG}} \times \frac{\text{TTr}}{\text{DTG}} = \frac{6 \times 60}{60} \times \frac{100}{40} = 15° \text{ Port}$$

Now for the limitations. Any distance off Tr. Req. means that the 'Distance to Go' will be greater than the simple deduction of 'Distance Gone' from Total Track.

However this discrepancy only becomes a real problem when the DOT is considerable and adjustment is left until the latter stages of the journey. In the above example use of a protractor will show that the adjustment should in fact be around 14° to Port – this is because the 'Distance to Go' is in reality just over 42 nm.

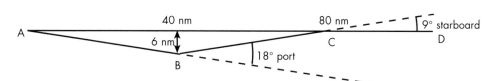

Figure 9.7

CHAPTER 9

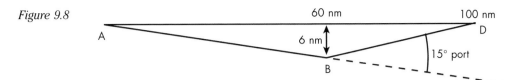

Figure 9.8

The 1-in-60 Rule and its uses can only be of partial help but certainly for adjustments made early in the flight – when they should be made – it can be most accurate. Try checking with a ruler and a protractor and you will be surprised at the accuracy.

The 10° Method

If you are averse to mental calculations there is another method you can use for heading corrections based on pure estimation on your part.

On your map draw lines at 10° to either side of your Tr. Req. line from the starting point and from the destination (Figure 9.9).

Figure 9.9

Suppose after a time you realise that you are off track and your position is pinpointed as X.

By simply making an educated estimate you can see this position X to be about 7° to starboard of your Tr. Req (Figure 9.10).

A change in heading of 7° to port will simply result in a track from X parallel to the Tr. Req.

However, you can also see that X is around 5° off Tr. Req. when related to the 10° line coming **from** the destination.

Add the two bearings together (7° + 5°) and an alteration in heading of 12° to Port will see you safely to your destination.

General Data

Indicated Airspeed (IAS)
– As shown on the airspeed indicator (ASI) is sufficient for microlight flying.

True Airspeed (TAS)
– The airspeed corrected for outside air temperature (OAT) using a computer.

Answers to Exercises on Page 143

Table 9.3

(i)	112° (M)	109° (C)
(ii)	232° (M)	234° (C)
(iii)	044° (M)	045° (C)
(iv)	163° (T)	166°(M)
(v)	337° (T)	335° (C)
(vi)	5° (W)	2° (E)

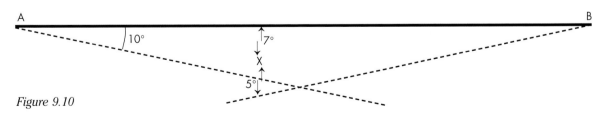

Figure 9.10

Chapter 10
Flight Planning and Map Reading

Map Reading

Flight planning starts with the selection of a suitable map or chart that will cover the area of the anticipated flight. It goes without saying that the map must be of the latest edition and therefore, not out of date.

At first glance, aeronautical maps may appear bewilderingly complex as they portray both the earth's surface and any overlying airspace. Familiarity is the secret to success; time spent studying the map and its associated information provides the best preparation.

Map reading in flight will progress with experience, but there are certain hints and tips worth knowing at the outset.

Maps Available

There are two main scales used in UK light aviation covering various regions of the country:

– The ¼ Million (Scale 1:250,000): 4 st. mls to 1" approx.

– The ½ Million (Scale 1:500,000): 8 st. mls to 1" approx.

The ¼ Million is able to show much more detail and at the speed and height a microlight aircraft travels there is time to absorb this detail. However, on the longer type of journey at above say 2000 ft the ½ Million with detail limited to major features would prove quite adequate and would also reduce the number of maps that had to be carried.

Two relevant points to note about these maps:

– The ½ Million shows **all** existing controlled airspace.

– The ¼ Million shows only controlled airspace from Surface to 5000 ft, but since being published in an entirely new presentation format it has begun to take over as the microlight pilot's favourite.

Should you choose to use the ¼ Million in the air you should still be in possession of the relevant ½ Million for planning purposes on the ground. There are other types of maps available but the above named two are sufficient for the time being.

Care of Maps

Ensure that any maps you choose have a glossy finish. This is essential to allow for the use of marker pens and subsequent erasure of any marks. The glossy finish also adds to the life span of the map, protecting it from dirt and the elements.

If a particular map you require is not available in the glossy finish, a covering of clear 'Fablon' will do the trick.

Whilst on the subject of protection, never leave your maps exposed to sunlight for any length of time. If you do, the colours will fade and important features such as hills and woods may not so easily be discerned.

Flight Planning
Pre-Flight Planning – Part 1

It goes without saying that you first assess the future weather from a forecast source in *Get Met*.

Microlights are now capable of travelling considerable distances and therefore more care is required in preparing for a journey than in the days when going 40 to 50 nm was a feat.

You should look up the details of your destination airfield in a flight guide. It is also necessary to access NOTAM and aeronautical information for your route as well as a final check for any temporary restricted airspace.

You plan to fly from A to B. Your first task is to draw in the Tr.Req. line on a ½ Million map and check for proximity to, or infringement of, controlled airspace and other 'taboo' zones.

Such controlled airspace may be above your intended altitude for the flight, but you should check that any factors such as high ground will not force you to climb to an altitude that would infringe such airspace. If so, then you must adjust the track line accordingly.

The code of the microlight pilot demands that adequate landing ground is always ahead and below.

By now the Tr.Req. line may no longer be a straight line but consist of several 'legs'. At least you can rest content that your chosen path is a safe one.

Flying allows freedom of movement in three dimensions, so as well as planning the lateral route (as we would in a car) we must also consider the vertical profile of the flight. The planned flight altitude will take into account weather conditions, elevation of proximate terrain/obstacles, nature of the terrain and controlled airspace. In the case of lowering cloud base or reducing visibility we must have calculated a minimum flight altitude below which we will not continue the flight.

Preparing a Flight Plan

Relying upon memory for a flight plan can be disastrous. Almost as bad, is scribbling pieces of vital information on a scrap of paper. The use of some planned type of form is highly recommended as reference to a flight plan in the air needs to be easy and instant.

The example of such a form shown in Figure 10.1 on page 152 should provide some food for thought.

In the process of working out headings you will also be in possession of other data, such as your groundspeed (GS) in relation to your planned airspeed (AS).

Knowing your groundspeed over each leg and the distance you have to cover, the time in air becomes a simple calculation allowing further planning.

1 Planned airspeed of 55 kt is calculated to give a 45 kt groundspeed.

2 Total track to be flown is 120 nm which at 45 kt means:

   Track/GS or 120/45 = 2 hrs 40 mins flying time.

3 Your fuel state allows for a cruise time of 2 hours (plus a suitable reserve eg 30min flying time) which would take you:

   GS × Flight Time or 45 × 2 = about 90 nm along track.

4 A re-fuelling stop is necessary after 75 or so nautical miles have been covered. This is playing it on the safe side to allow for you having used more power than intended and to allow a reserve for finding and landing at that stop.

Pre-Flight Planning – Part 2

Any scheduled re-fuelling stop must now be marked on the map with the nearest rather than the furthest suitable site being selected within the mileage range necessary.

The next step is to establish 'waypoints' on your Tr.Req. Waypoints are easily identifiable features marked at intervals on the map which when sighted confirm that you are on track or not as the case may be.

In the absence of a compass it is essential that they be close enough together for the next one to be in view from the present one.

At the outset and at every change of heading, double up on the waypoints you mark – later you will see the value of so doing.

Figure 10.1 Example of a cross-country flight plan form

MICROLIGHT AIRCRAFT
CROSS-COUNTRY FLIGHT PLAN

Date:	Route:						Height AMSL
Name:	Out Landings:						
Aircraft type:	Reg. QNH						
Reg. No.							
F/cast from:	Dir.	Vel.	Time of forecast:				
Wind at 2000 ft			Turbulence		Vis.	Cloud/Base	
Est. for 1000 ft							
Est. for 500 ft							

LEG	Tr. Req.	Est. Drift	Var.	Hdg. Mag.	Dist.	GS	Time
NOTES: (Waypoints, Landmarks, High Ground, etc.)					Min Flt Alt	Planned Flt Alt	Altim Adj't

LEG	Tr. Req.	Est. Drift	Var.	Hdg. Mag.	Dist.	GS	Time
NOTES: (Waypoints, Landmarks, High Ground, etc.)					Min Flt Alt	Planned Flt Alt	Altim Adj't

LEG	Tr. Req.	Est. Drift	Var.	Hdg. Mag.	Dist.	GS	Time
NOTES: (Waypoints, Landmarks, High Ground, etc.)					Min Flt Alt	Planned Flt Alt	Altim Adj't

LEG	Tr. Req.	Est. Drift	Var.	Hdg. Mag.	Dist.	GS	Time
NOTES: (Waypoints, Landmarks, High Ground, etc.)					Min Flt Alt	Planned Flt Alt	Altim Adj't

ALTIMETER SETTING FOR QFE AT DESTINATION

If no pressure-setting scale, **set height amsl** on take-off. On arrival overhead, reduce altimeter reading by the height amsl of destination to give a 0 ft reading on landing (QFE).

E.g. Enstone 550 ft to Wellesbourne 160ft. Set 550 ft on take-off.
   Overhead Wellesbourne, reduce reading by 160 ft.
   On landing, altimeter reading will be 0 ft (QFE).

For a few nautical miles' radius around your destination, ring that spot with additional marked features. You may assess that you have reached your journey's end to find that it is not there. Having made it thus far it is reasonable to assume that your goal cannot be far away. With your destination ringed with marked features within a '**circle of uncertainty**' you will be in a much better position to sort yourself out.

Should you have worked out your speeds accurately and feel that you can stick to them in the air then your waypoints can be fixed at regular time intervals of say 5 minutes flight duration between each. Here you have the advantage of checking the progress you are making in terms of groundspeed.

Nearer the take-off time your concentration should again be on your weather forecast – checking its time is still valid in your *Get Met* booklet. As mentioned in covering met, use should be made of METARs and TAFs, but care should be taken if their source is not your specific destination.

Ideally, when this is the case, a phone call to your intended destination is essential even if Prior Permission Required (PPR) is not necessary.

Satellite Navigation (Sat Nav)

If ever an aid to navigation has made an impact on pilots it is Satellite Navigation (Sat Nav) – it is both affordable and attractive. Hence it is being discussed to ensure you clearly understand that it is **a back-up, not a bible**. It must only be a support to your written flight plan/map; you must never use it in isolation.

How it works is left to the instructions accompanying your type of Sat Nav; you should follow them carefully. However, just a few tips would not be out of place:

– Plan your flight as previously described. The availability of a Sat Nav does not reduce the need for careful planning; in fact it increases the amount of time likely to be spent on pre-flight preparations.

– Set up your Sat Nav ensuring that the waypoints are entered correctly. Ensure that the tracks and distances between waypoints contained in the Sat Nav route are the same as those recorded on your flight plan.

– Be fully aware that major problems arise from mistakes in the initial input.

– It is far from easy to make adjustments to your Sat Nav once you are airborne – particularly if you wear gloves.

– At the risk of repetition, it must ever remain as a back-up – a brilliant one at that. The American satellites combine to produce the most frequently used Global Positioning System (GPS). So your motto must always be: '**eyeball and map first, global positioning second**'. Always think of the 'S' in 'GPS' as standing for 'second'.

Ask those who chose the easy option what happened when a faulty input was made and/or when the batteries ran out in flight. Yes, sadly it has happened – with the most serious consequences on occasion.

Map Reading in Flight

How you secure your map in flight for easy reference is a matter for your own ingenuity and initiative. Some pilots like to have the map 'the right way up' – others like to orientate it so that they are flying along the track line with features coming up on the ground as they appear on the map. The choice is yours.

Having taken off, climb to a position central to your take-off point, which in essence is the start of your Tr.Req. line, and adopt your planned heading at the same time checking it for accuracy. This you do by positioning your aircraft so that the doubled up waypoints referred to earlier are in line with each other. Once this picture is set up check that your planned heading matches it – if not, adopt the new heading, make a note of it and stick to it for that leg.

You are now sure of being on your Tr.Req. and have allowed for any drift. Adopt the same procedure for each leg as a new heading becomes necessary.

Hints and Tips

Assuming you are now confidently on your way it is time to take note of a few hints and tips.

Waypoints

- Make sure the main selected waypoints marked on your map also take into account other features around them. It is no good spotting an 'expected' TV mast if it is the wrong one. Checking that those additional features are also present confirms your scheduled waypoint.

- Again, if you spot an unexpected feature on your track which is not on your map – check the date of your map. New buildings and roads can appear quite quickly.

Features

- The higher you go the less obvious becomes that hill you find hard to struggle up on foot.

- Main roads which you know like the back of your hand as a motorist can be obscured from the air by foliage when lined with trees.

- Secondary roads with shallow hedging, or no hedging at all can easily be mistaken for main roads due to the clarity with which they stand out. This would particularly apply when over the Fenland.

- Railway lines across country are fine but close to a town they usually multiply and can lead to confusion.

- Disused railway lines are excellent as they are invariably untended and therefore stand out like scars in an otherwise orderly agricultural surround.

- Woods are very useful but the Forestry Commission do fell trees from time to time so ensure your map is up to date.

- Motorways, new bypasses and dual carriageways can quickly make a map out of date. Ensure you do not become confused at sighting newly constructed ones which are so prevalent around new towns.

Cloud Shadow

- The shadow cast on the ground by a cloud can quickly obliterate that all important waypoint you expect to see come up on schedule. Cope with this by an intermediate check of features which should be around but not marked down during your preparation.

Sun

- The sun in your eyes, particularly on a hazy day, can play havoc with your forward visibility. Anticipate this possibility by increasing the number of marked waypoints before you start. This is also a good move for a hazy/misty day when the sun is not so dominant.

Sun Spots

- Far ahead you see your destination clearly, basking in a pool of sunlight between shadows. If your concentration is not up to the mark you may find yourself heading for that pool of sunlight which will, of course, be moving away from your destination at the speed of the wind at cloud level. By all means use the sighting far ahead but only to line up with a known waypoint to confirm your current heading or to initiate a change of heading if it is warranted.

Temperature inversions

- These are associated with anticyclones that may produce a clear blue sky above but an inversion may produce haze. You might consider the visibility reasonable from the ground but you may not have to climb very high to find the ground ahead disappearing and your next landmark out of sight.

No doubt you will find out many other such 'wrinkles' for yourself, proving that map reading is very much a practical art rather than a theoretical one.

Dealing with Problems

There are times when to be realistic about it, you come across problems. Your engine is playing up or for some other reason you cannot maintain your planned height and the possibility of a precautionary landing must be considered.

The lower you are the less time you have to select a field in the event of needing one. In this situation it is essential that you are governed by common sense and not a blind adherence to your planned track. Deviate from the track where necessary to ensure that any given moment you have a safe landing ground below you without having to rely on any normal gliding time to reach it. This is not to say that there is not a need to fly at all times with an unscheduled landing in mind. It is simply a matter of when the problem arises low down the choice is drastically reduced. Unscheduled landings need an assessment to be made of wind direction. It would be sad to 'bend' your aircraft through a crosswind touch-down when conditions were otherwise ideal.

Smoke has traditionally been the life-saver in the past but today there is little of it about to show up a wind direction. One such aid can be ripples across water. A stretch of water sheltered by trees or a high bank at one end will show a calm patch of water at that sheltered end.

Cloud shadow moving across the ground is another aid, but remember to aim around 30° to the **left** of the shadow's track as you turn into wind – the shadow's movement will be more in line with the geostrophic wind direction than that of the surface wind.

All in all, your safest move is to monitor any indication of wind direction at intervals during the flight and not leave it until a problem arises.

Probably the greatest hazard you will ever have to face in landing out is that of power lines. The wires or cables themselves are unlikely to be seen until the last minute and certainly not from any reasonable height. However, the pylons or poles supporting them are certainly visible if you care to keep a careful look-out so whenever you see two poles always assume them to be joined by a cable.

Not to be recommended is flying under power lines, but in the course of driving about the countryside you should take note of the cable heights in relation to the types of pylons/poles in terms of size. There is more to be said for

passing underneath than for stalling-in on the top of this hazard.

In the case of deteriorating weather conditions, low fuel state, the approach of darkness, a sick passenger or any other situation requiring landing sooner rather than later, a diversion to an alternative landing site should be considered. If time permits a landing at one of your 'planned' alternative sites will be preferable to completing a precautionary landing. Indeed, an early decision to divert to an alternative landing site will invariably negate the need for a precautionary landing to be commmpleted later!

Finally, should you be lost, there is always the sun. If the time is around midday, drop downuntil your shadow is visible on the ground and with the knowledge that the sun will be to the south at that time you should be able to obtain a reasonable check on your heading. If the shadow is to the right, you are going west; shadow to left, you are going east; shadow in front, you are going north. You should not need to be told in what direction you are heading when the sun is directly in front.

When lost in the proximity of controlled airspace unless you are quite sure that you can quickly re-establish your position in a very short space of time then land at once and find out exactly where you are. At least a microlight allows you this facility, denied to most other aviators, and it is better to be safe than sorry.

If your aircraft is equipped with radio make contact with an ATC Unit as soon as possible and explain your situaution. The controller is there to help you and has many facilities at his/her disposal to assist in resolving the situation.

Map reading can be a very rewarding task. There is a tremendous satisfaction to be had as well as safety in knowing that you are where you planned to be at all times.

Index